RESEARCHING AND WRITING HISTORY

RESEARCHING AND WRITING HISTORY

A Practical Guide for Local Historians

David Dymond

BRITISH ASSOCIATION FOR LOCAL HISTORY

Published by the British Association for Local History
24 Lower Street, Harnham, SALISBURY, SP2 8EY

ISBN 1 86077 115 7

First edition 1999

(BALH General Editor: Alan G. Crosby)

Cover illustration: the background detail, reproduced with the kind permission
of the Ordnance Survey, is from the One-Inch District Map of Liverpool 1927;
the photograph shows the wedding of Alexander Bagshaw and May Routledge
in Openshaw, Manchester, 18 October 1922.

Set in Palatino

Designed, printed and bound by
Smith Settle Limited, Ilkley Road, OTLEY, LS21 3JP

LIST OF CONTENTS

- -

FIGURES

FACSIMILES, TRANSCRIPTS & ANALYSES

To my three children, Catherine, Eleanor and Charles
With love and apologies for dragging them into so many churches

ABBREVIATIONS

JORALS	*Journal of Regional & Local Studies*
LHM	*The Local History Magazine*
LPS	*Local Population Studies*
PRO	Public Record Office (Kew, London)
TLH	*The Local Historian*
VCH	*Victoria County History*

FOREWORD

In recent years I have been embarrassed that this book — which first appeared in 1981 under the title *Writing Local History* — was still being reprinted and sold. It was obviously out-of-date and needed substantial revision. Since 1981 we have witnessed many important developments including a boom in family history, new academic initiatives within local history, significant new publications, a sharp increase in the number of dissertations being written, and on top of everything else the word-processing and computing revolution. As the number of people seeking advice in this field is still growing, and no rival title has appeared, the only honest response was to re-think and re-write the whole book.

As was said in the Foreword to the first edition, I do not propose to discuss historical sources in any detail, or to introduce special techniques like palaeography, record-linkage and computing. A number of publications already give good advice on such subjects, and more will undoubtedly appear. Nor, at the other end of the subject, am I much concerned with the business of getting into print, though many people would certainly value up-to-date practical help with the new technologies of commercial and desk-top publishing. The central purpose remains, as before, to investigate how we discipline ourselves to write better. This inevitably means thinking about the earlier processes of research as well, a point which is conceded in the revised title of the book. In other words, how do we find and analyse evidence and then convert our thoughts, through our pens or word-processors, into a reasoned yet imaginative reconstruction of the past?

THE BOOK'S ARRANGEMENT

The main text has been subdivided into twelve self-contained sections, so that the reader can quickly find what he or she wants. To emphasise particularly important points, some sentences have been italicised to catch the eye of those who are skimming. The index on p. 162 should also help readers to find their way around. The first chapter discusses the state of Local History at the end of the 20th century, while chapters 2-9 deal with the various stages of practical research and writing. It should be borne in mind that these stages often merge, overlap and are done concurrently. In the final 70 pages of the book, 22 appendices provide more detailed information, examples of writing and practical exercises. Originally produced as teaching-aids they will, I hope, have value for a range of actual and would-be writers, and provide teachers at various levels with ideas which are worth adapting to their own circumstances.

I hope that readers will not find too many flaws and inconsistencies in the following pages. The danger of writing a didactic work of this kind is that one risks breaking recommendations and rules as one makes them. Any comments and criticisms which might lead to the improvement of later reprints will be gratefully received.

ACKNOWLEDGEMENTS

In revising this book I have received invaluable help and advice from many friends and colleagues, though they must not be held responsible for any errors or for the opinions expressed. In particular I would like to mention the following: Stella Colwell, Claire Cross, Gordon Forster, Evelyn Lord, John Marshall, Lionel Munby, Peter Northeast, Clive Paine, Alan Rogers, Ted Royle and Kate Tiller. Alan Crosby, the general editor of BALH, has been particularly generous with his time, giving me copious and stimulating comments as the book took shape. Finally I wish to express my gratitude to numerous local historians whom I have met over more than thirty years in adult classes, residential courses, local societies, county committees and in the British Association for Local History. They have pointed out defects in the first edition of 1981, and raised issues which I then overlooked. Above all it is they who have convinced me that local history is much more than an academic subject and that its real potential, for individuals and for society as a whole, has yet to be realised.

CONFESSION

Unfortunately the English language has no singular pronoun covering male and female, a fact which probably casts shame on Anglo-Saxon and Middle-English attitudes. So normally I have been forced to refer to the local historian as 'he'. Endless repetition of the only real alternatives (such as 'he or she', 'she or he', 'he/she') would have been tedious to all readers. In acknowledgement of this verbal injustice, I wish to assert here that women are *at least* as important as men in this branch of history — just as they were in the past itself.

DAVID DYMOND
Bury St Edmunds
July 1999

'I have confessed to you that I am fond of local histories. It is the general execution of them that I condemn, and that I call *the worst kind of reading.* I cannot comprehend but that they might be performed with taste.'
(Horace Walpole in letter to Rev William Cole, 1780)

'But a new intensity of investigation has forced the narrowing of the geographical and spatial horizon. As we shall see, instead of the majestic sweep through hundreds of years of European history, we are confined often to one English county, or even one village.'
(Alan Macfarlane, *Witchcraft in Tudor and Stuart England*, 1970, p. 5)

'Eventually indeed, when the history of English towns and villages has been written as it ought to be, the study of English history itself will also be revolutionised.'
(Alan Everitt, *Ways and Means in Local History*, 1971, p. 5)

'What distinguishes a significant from an insignificant piece of historical research is not the size of the unit of investigation, whether in time or space, but the ends in view and the methods used.'
(E. A. Wrigley, *The Local and the General in Population History*, 1985, p. 1)

'I have always believed that through local history we can develop a new version of national history: local history should never simply illustrate national history, or take it as given, it should point to new interpretations.'
(Asa Briggs, foreword to G. Mayhew, *Tudor Rye* , 1987)

'A good national history of inclosure will refer to Widmerpool [Notts.] or other places in order to show how real people were affected. A good local history of the inclosure of Widmerpool will show that what happened there was part of a national pattern, not a wholly unique experience.'
(Christopher Lewis, *Particular Places*, BL, 1989, p. 48)

'In our mobile society, in which many people do not look to traditional institutions to provide stability, local knowledge helps us to 'dig in', to become rooted in a place, rather than perching unconnected and uninvolved.'
(Carol Kammen, *History News*, 50, 3, 1995)

'But local history is frequently the nursery for ideas that are developed on the national stage, its seeds are germinated into the lawns of history.'
(William Gibson in *Archives*, xxiii, no.98, Apr. 1998, 68)

SIR WILLIAM DUGDALE, 1605-86, Garter King of Arms, pioneering antiquary and local historian, whose writings include *Antiquities of Warwickshire* (1656), *The History of St Paul's Cathedral* (1658) and the monumental *Monasticon Anglicanum* (with Roger Dodsworth, 1655-61). Looking at this portrait, modern historians and archivists can only boggle at the chaotic table and shelves, the use of ink beside original documents, and the need to write history with a hat on! Today's researchers expect high standards of conservation and use sophisticated technology, but the basic intellectual responsibilities are much the same as in earlier generations. Our constant task as historians is to think both critically and imaginatively, and to write with lucidity and elegance.

(Drawn and engraved by Wenceslaus Hollar, 1655)

1. THE PRESENT STATE OF LOCAL HISTORY

Local history is difficult to define. It can be viewed as an emphasis within the broad spectrum of historical studies, at the opposite end from world history because it deals with human life in a detailed, microscopic way. Local historians claim to study the lives of the great mass of humanity — 'ordinary' people, 'the common run of chaps', in 'little' places like individual towns and villages. In that sense their work is akin to those sciences which deal with the smallest and most fundamental bits of life and matter. An even wider coverage can, however, be postulated. 'Top people' such as royalty and statesmen, who today are normally excluded from local history because of their national and international importance, also had (or should have had) private and *localised* lives.[1] So alternatively one might argue that local history is concerned with localities and local communities: it is the study of local people, as individuals but particularly as groups, in the places where they lived, worked and died.[2] But with any choice of language new problems arise. Where does 'local' begin and end, who or what is 'ordinary', and what exactly is a 'community'? Seeking more precision we can argue for ever over these slippery words, but local history does not have, and can never have, exact limits. It overlaps substantially with family and population history, and merges with other approaches to the past such as landscape, economic, business, urban, social and cultural history.

Definable or not, local history is widely pursued for its own rewards, and has been repeatedly justified by academics as having a value in its own right.[3] As we

---

[1] For C. Phythian-Adams, English local history 'is concerned with nothing less than the entire English people': *Societies, Cultures and Kinship, 1580-1850* (1993), pp. xi-xii. Interestingly, old-style parish and town histories often devoted considerable space to 'worthies' — eminent individuals of more than local significance.

[2] 'Local history has two essential ingredients — people and place. Together they have interacted to produce changing, but particular, historical experiences in the many differing areas of England': Kate Tiller, *English Local History: An Introduction* (1992), p. 1; '[Local history] is the story of people in small social groups living in one place rather than another': Christopher Lewis, *Particular Places* (1989),p. 9. However, 'people' and 'place' are not equally important *objects* of study, as some people persist in thinking when they confuse Local History with Landscape History. 'For the local historian, his subject is not a place, a village, parish or town, but a group of people': Alan Rogers, *Approaches to Local History* (1977), p. 6.

[3] For example, H. P. R. Finberg & V. H. T. Skipp, *Local History, Objective and Pursuit* (1967), p. 32; C. Phythian-Adams, *Re-thinking English Local History* (Leicester UP, 1987), p. 2.

reach the millennium nobody can doubt the enthusiasm and industry shown by a wide range of practitioners. Record offices and local-studies libraries have never been fuller, more sources are being searched and more evidence discovered than ever before, new societies and journals are still being founded, and the tide of publication seems to rise remorselessly. It is now generally agreed that York and Lavenham are no more 'historical' than Cleethorpes and Battersea, for 'everywhere has an interesting past'.[1] Most encouraging of all is the fact that new converts to the subject, of widely differing ages, are still appearing in every corner of Britain. Unlike earlier generations, children today are lucky enough to be introduced to local history at school, although its scope and depth depend heavily on the confidence and preparedness of individual teachers.[2]

In practice local historians amass information and ideas which test, refine and sometimes contradict the broader generalisations of those working at a 'higher' (usually national) level.[3] Furthermore they frequently discover entirely new themes which have the potential to become national. For example, as a pioneering local historian W. G. Hoskins was one of the first to draw attention to the value of investigating regional surnames and vernacular buildings: both studies are now specialisations in their own right. In this sense the word 'microcosmic' might seem a better description of local history than 'microscopic'.[4] The influences, however, are not simply one-way. While deeply involved in his chosen field, the perceptive local historian by wide reading absorbs the ideas of other historical specialists. These upward and downward trends mean that *local history and national history are utterly dependent on each other: they perpetually collide in a creative way, illuminating and transforming each other.*

The effect of local history on the individual is not myopic, as some would claim, but can be genuinely liberating. As Alan Everitt has argued, 'the study of local history can both broaden the mind and deepen the sympathies in very much the same way as travelling in a distant country'.[5] It enables us to avoid the modern danger of feeling detached from our human and physical environment, and to dig ourselves into a community consisting not only of the living but of the countless

---

[1] Lewis, *Particular Places*, p. 9.

[2] It also depends on the extent to which help is available from archivists, librarians and education officers. The National Curriculum currently specifies thirteen Study Units for pupils aged from five to fourteen years: only one *must* be an exercise in local history, but seven others *could* involve local evidence and examples. Changes to the curriculum, being proposed from 2000, will probably give fewer opportunities for studying local history.

[3] Using a different metaphor, Margaret Bonney talks of the local historian's opportunity 'to muddy the water': *TLH*, 24, 1 (1994), 2-3.

[4] M. M. Postan, *Essays on Historical Method* (1971), 20-1.

[5] Alan Everitt, *Ways and means in Local History* (NCSS, 1971), p. 50. John Marshall has similarly talked of 'the most magnificent liberal education' afforded by local and regional history: *The Amateur Historian* 6, 1 (Autumn 1963), 11-17.

dead. As a consequence, our lives acquire more meaning and a deeper perspective. Moreover, although this factor is not recognised widely enough, local history has considerable social and communal value. It can, for example, help to break down educational and class barriers by bringing together people of different ages and backgrounds. Its effect is particularly strong when practical recording and elementary research are being undertaken: witness the understanding and human warmth generated when schoolchildren interview the elderly. The end-product can be genuine 'People's History', sometimes leading to 'Community Publishing'; both are initiatives which deserve to be treated with respect.[1]

It follows that the subject has political importance, for local knowledge undoubtedly helps to make grass-root democracy more informed, sensitive and effective. Although the pace of modern change is frenzied, citizens are more likely to be aware of their own cultural and environmental 'heritage' and are better able to defend it if they have access to good, de-mythologised local history — on matters such as landscape, vernacular architecture, dialect, place-names, agricultural history, traditional industries, customs, leisure patterns, religious traditions, and the lives of individuals.[2] It is no exaggeration to say that, when sound localised research is completed and made public, the life of the relevant human group can never be quite the same again — because it now knows more about itself and its place in the wider world. In Europe generally, the new interest in political devolution and 'subsidiarity' will in part depend on a deepening public consciousness of local and regional character, and on the successful identification of human communities, large and small, past and contemporary.[3] In these and other ways, *local history should be regarded not just as an academic subject, important though that is, but as a form of public knowledge which will be increasingly deployed in the social and political debates of the 21st century.*[4]

[1] L. Sitzia, 'QueenSpark Books: Publishing Life Histories for the Local Community', *TLH*, 27, 4 (Nov. 1997), 218-24. Nigel Morgan investigated working-class housing in 19th-century Preston; with his wife's help he published three books and found that one of his best outlets was 'the Spar shop down the road': *LHM*, 44 (May-June 1994), 9-13. This research is now being re-published by an American university press.
[2] For 60 years the Enfield Preservation Society has done voluntary work, published local history and applied political pressure: V. Carter, *Fighting for the Future: The Study of Enfield Preservation Society, 1936-96* (Enfield Pres. Soc., 1997). Kate Gilbert's *Life in a Hampshire Village: The History of Ashley* (Hants CC, 1992) was commissioned after a successful campaign to save a Norman church from de-consecration 'so that in future no one would underrate its [Ashley's] historical interest'. In 1979 widespread protest at local and national level greeted the government's decision to sell the open-field manor of Laxton, Notts; eventually the estate was sold for less than half its market value to the Crown Estates Commissioners who undertook to continue the medieval system: J. V. Beckett, *A History of Laxton: England's Last Open-Field Village* (1989), pp. 6-7.
[3] For a good example of a local historian contributing to this debate, see John Chandler, *A Sense of Belonging: History, Community and the New Wiltshire* (1998).
[4] Alan Rogers argues strongly that 'local history belongs to the people and should be restored to them — not just by the presentation of the findings of scholars through public lectures but by opening the doors to the people to research their own past': *JORALS*, 15, 1 (Summer 1995), 1-14. Dennis Mills appeals for the writing of 'outline histories' of individual parishes: *TLH*, 24, 4 (Nov. 1994), 225-8.

Academics often complain about the antiquarianism of ordinary local historians, and their failure to engage with broader ideas.[1] They unfairly refuse to judge the subject by its successes, and by what it offers large numbers of people actually and potentially. They fail to see that popular local history, for all its wastefulness and unpredictability, promotes a great deal of activity, opens up new subjects, releases new knowledge and, most important of all, constantly unearths new talent. We should applaud the broad amateur base of local history, and not regard it with regret or embarrassment. In every region of Britain individuals and groups are fired by the desire to learn more about their localities, and indeed to make their own contribution. These are, in Kate Tiller's useful phrase, 'local local historians'.[2] They are not too troubled by definitions and theories, but 'are all determined to get on with it!'[3] This is a popular, practical and empirical approach to the past which develops out of a natural fascination with those aspects of life which are close, familiar and 'everyday'. It is normal to see local historians beavering away in libraries and record offices, attending lectures and guided excursions as members of local societies, and undertaking courses as adult students. From such activities, they obviously derive considerable pleasure and profit: exploring the dimension of time with its multiple layers, and probing into the lives of those who preceded them in a particular place. They enjoy the thrills of unearthing evidence, of questioning and detection, and of using their eyes to delve behind surface appearances. Not infrequently such explorations lead to the production of books and other forms of publication, which find a ready market among both residents and visitors.[4]

Wanting to go further, but not necessarily wishing to become fully professional, a minority of activists now seek formal historical training; they form an important middle group between full-time academics and 'local local historians'. The sharp rise in the number of adult students acquiring credits and other qualifications such as certificates, diplomas, first degrees and higher degrees, and the resultant accumulation of dissertations and theses, promises a steady increase in the volume of good-quality research, publishing and teaching. Indeed, at meetings of activists nowadays (for example, at seminars and conferences) it is often difficult to distinguish full-timers from part-timers, academics from laymen. What really matters on these occasions is the quality of the history being discussed, not the status of the proponent.[5]

---

[1] K. Schurer, 'The Future for Local History: Boom or Recession?', *TLH*, 21, 3 (Aug. 1991), 99-108.
[2] Kate Tiller, *English Local History: The State of the Art* (University of Cambridge Board of Continuing Education, Occasional Papers, 1, 1998).
[3] *Report of the Committee to Review Local History* [Blake Report], (1979), p. 2.
[4] The only attempt to assess the activities of local historians nationally came in the early 1980s, when David Hayns wrote his reports as Field Officer of BALH: see *Field Officer's Report* (BALH, 1982-3, 1983-4). In 1983 Hayns also produced *Local History in Norfolk and Suffolk — A Preliminary Survey*.
[5] The contrast with the 19th century could not be more dramatic, for then local history was largely the preserve of the gentry, clergy and leisured classes.

Nobody can deny, however, that local history has its problems, mainly because of uneven standards and internal division. Obvious examples are the corruptions and myths perpetrated by those whose motives are mainly commercial, and who therefore put entertainment before education. Many of us cringe when we encounter feeble or phoney history in newspapers, magazines and local television, or witness the silliest excesses of the burgeoning 'heritage industry' when people dress up as monks, minstrels or Roman legionaries.[1] I particularly abominate ghost and graveyard trails in great cities like York and Birmingham. Undemanding pap of this kind is not merely irritating, but makes the genuine historian's task more difficult.

For most of the problems, however, we can only blame ourselves.[2] It is sadly true that various interest-groups within local history tend to ignore each other as they blithely pursue their own priorities. Rifts still exist between academics and antiquarians, between parochialists and regionalists, between those who prefer short chronologies and those who prefer long. Few would deny that contacts are weak between those who focus on early periods (medieval) and those whose interests are later (early modern, modern, and contemporary); between those who study documents and those concerned with landscapes and artefacts; between those who investigate rural areas and those who work on towns or large industrial conurbations.[3] Of course variety in one sense invigorates the subject, and in practice individuals and groups regularly cross most of those boundaries. Nevertheless, only a few local historians seem prepared to discuss objectives, standards and co-operation. Finberg's judgement of 1964 remains broadly true, that 'local history still suffers from a lack of theoretical discussion'.[4] Hence much local research and writing is not as comparative and cumulative as it should be, and effort is unnecessarily wasted. Obviously we still need to improve the channels of communication between local historians of all kinds — at local, regional and national levels.[5]

One of the most serious divides has been between the local and family approaches. As a great popular movement family history is relatively modern, yet in two to three decades the number of active family historians has grown far beyond that of

---

[1] Edward Royle has recently referred to the 'vapid commercial candy-floss of the heritage industry': *TLH*, 28, 3 (Aug. 1998), 178.

[2] To some commentators, the situation is so bad that 'the empire of local history is in decay and it is time to rally round its flag': Lewis, *Particular Places*, p. 8. In certain regions, the idea that local history is in crisis is founded on dwindling numbers of adult classes, on the precarious existence of some local societies, and on the comparative boom in Family History.

[3] As in other walks of life, the country is divided north-south. Perhaps we should encourage local societies to twin: why shouldn't, say, the Petworth Hist. Soc. have links with the Gateshead Antiquarians? Voluntary societies have a lot to learn from each other.

[4] H. P. R. Finberg, *Local History in the University* (Leicester UP, 1964), p. 16.

[5] We can all profit from reading the works of leading academic theorists such as Phythian-Adams and Marshall, though some would regard their influence as more divisive than unifying. BALH as the one charity dealing with local history nationally must clearly take some responsibility and become a more effective mediator through its publications and activities.

local historians. At first the two groups were suspicious of each other, although their interests obviously overlap (families and kinship are basic to any kind of social history, and no individual or family can be understood without reference to a community and society). For example, local historians tended to regard family historians as mere name-hunters, ancestor-worshippers and constructors of family-trees, who were noisy and took up too much space in local record offices. Slowly, however, the two groups are showing a willingness to live together, to learn from each other, and even to merge their interests. One of best symbols of this is the work of Dr David Hey of Sheffield University who is the only person to have held an academic chair in Local and Family History.[1] The influence of the Local Population Studies Society and of the Open University through courses like DA301 has also helped many activists to get beyond the mere collecting of names and family-trees, and to find out about how life was actually lived in the family and other social groupings.[2] In the course of personal development a good family historian will inevitably become a local historian — and *vice versa*. Even if progress is slow, we must hope that the two subjects continue to overlap and fuse.[3]

Another highly significant divide is between full-time academics and part-time 'amateurs'.[4] Since the Second World War the study of local history has been galvanised, and to some extent confused, by the influence of academic historians. These have included a relatively small number of specialist local historians ('general local historians'!), mainly working in university departments of history or continuing education,[5] and a much larger group of university-based professionals who, while not calling themselves local historians, use local history in the investigation of broader themes. Both groups have repeatedly castigated amateur local history for being descriptive, uncritical, anecdotal and rose-tinted, in short 'antiquarian'. These were the criticisms, for example, when in the mid-1960s a vigorous controversy broke out in the pages of *The Amateur Historian*.[6] The argument has rumbled on ever since,

---

[1] See David Hey, *Family History and Local History in England* (Longman, 1987); C. D. Rogers & J. H. Smith, *Local Family History in England* (Manchester UP, 1991).

[2] Such approaches also carry dangers: for example, a narrowness caused by the lack of experience and background knowledge, and too great a fascination with methodology and new technology.

[3] Some have argued the opposite. 'Local history societies have opened their doors to family historians, to the extent that there is a danger that the difference between the two may be becoming increasingly blurred': N. Goose, *Archives*, xxii, 97 (Oct. 1997), 101.

[4] I am using the word 'professional' to mean a full-time specialist employed in an academic institution, and not to imply that such a person produces work which is necessarily superior. Similarly I use 'amateur' to mean a dedicated part-timer. When it comes to standards, surprising and unexpected differences can be found in both camps.

[5] The only Department of English Local History, founded in 1952, is at Leicester University. Elsewhere the main development in the last generation has been the establishment of centres of regional studies, as at Lancaster, Keele, Exeter and UEA. It is now vital that these centres are not emasculated or destroyed by financial cuts.

[6] *The Amateur Historian*, vol. 6, Nos 1, 2, 4, 6, 7, 8 (1963-4).

and received another boost in 1997 with the publication of John Marshall's *Tyranny of the Discrete*.[1]

The basic charge is undoubtedly correct. Published local histories are often uncritical, shapeless and anecdotal, relying heavily on miscellaneous and undigested bits of evidence. They are frequently nostalgic in tone, tending to overstress stability and to neglect change and conflict. Local communities were *not* always stable and harmonious, for many rifts and realignments were caused by new economic, social or religious trends.[2] Another justified criticism is that local historians often ignore the inward and outward movement of both people and influences, and overlook those links with the outside world which help to make sense of what is found locally.[3] They give the impression that the locality being studied is unique and self-contained — in fact 'the centre of the universe'. In other words, the parish boundary has become a mental barrier, an intellectual Berlin Wall. In fact, one's community or locality can only be properly understood when it is viewed as a significant part of the wider world. The choice has been very clearly described by David Hey:

> Nothing is more difficult for a local historian who is deeply immersed in all the minutiae of the history of his particular place than to raise his sights beyond the local boundaries, so as to place his findings in a wider context. Only by being aware of what is happening elsewhere will he understand what is special and what is typical about his chosen subject.[4]

On the other hand, to be fair, these dangers are now more widely recognised, and have been stressed by most of those teaching local history in the last generation. *At its best*, the writing of non-professional local history is no longer 'amateurish': it is indeed critical, comparative and cumulative, just as critics have long demanded.[5] Furthermore, it is increasing in volume as a result of newer developments, such as the proliferation of certificates and masters' degrees.

In the last thirty years, academic local historians have vigorously promoted two major concepts which are related but should never be confused. The first, as mentioned in the last paragraph, stresses the value of historical context. *Whatever* his chosen territory, be it a single parish or a large industrial region, the local historian must

---

[1] J. D. Marshall, *The Tyranny of the Discrete: A Discussion of the Problems of Local History in England* (Scolar, 1997). See David Hey's review of this book in *TLH*, 28, 2 (May 1998), 123-4.

[2] See K. Wrightson, *English Society, 1580-1680* (1982), esp. chs 6 & 7. Ironically, those who advocate 'community history' tend to accept the administrative units presented by their sources, and give little time to the discussion of alternative and equally real communities.

[3] Local histories usually have titles like *A History of Ambridge* or *The Book of Borchester*, whereas professional studies, though based on single local communities, often make wider claims under titles like *The Midland Peasant* or *The Making of an Industrial Society*.

[4] Review in *TLH*, 30, 3 (Nov. 1990), 141.

[5] To justify the coinage of a new term, Dennis Mills very unfairly equated all bad practice with *local* history and all good with *community* history: *Getting into Community History* (LPSS 1995), pp. 7-16. He even implied that 'the typical local historian' prefers to study 'important' people.

always put it into a broader setting and thereby acknowledge the flow of influences in and out. Any territory should in particular be related 'to the broader area or areas immediately above it'.[1] This awareness of the outside world can be gained in various ways: for example, by looking at wide-ranging primary sources such as tax returns and census abstracts, by conscientiously reading other historians' work, and by consulting data collected in major research projects (those, for example, estimating the populations of smaller English towns at various dates, or mapping Hearth Tax returns on a national scale).[2]

The second concept is Regional History which emphasises that previous generations had mental horizons much wider than the individual parish, township or manor. For centuries people of all social levels, for a whole variety of reasons, walked and rode beyond their local boundaries, and thereby forged broader links, affinities and allegiances. Regions in this sense can vary greatly in size, and need not be permanent; they are not necessarily defined by administrative boundaries, and are certainly not spaces chosen for the personal convenience of historians. Larger-scale examples can include the economic hinterlands of great cities, areas dominated by particular industries, distinctive countrysides or 'pays' with their own characteristic types of farming, large landed estates whether unified or scattered, and 'provinces' dependent on major drainage-systems. On a smaller scale, one can talk of 'neighbourhoods' centring on the household of a particular landlord (e.g. Stiffkey in Norfolk), or of 'societies' defined by the dominance of certain 'core families' (e.g. south-west Nottinghamshire).[3] This approach forces us to think much more carefully about the definition of 'communities', and about the characteristics which linked and divided people in the past. It also makes us realise that regions can be purely personal, mental concepts, varying over time according to factors like wealth, education, leisure and the ability to travel.[4] For all its theoretical and intellectual attraction to professionals, however, regional history must be recognised as difficult to write, not often achieved and, at present, not as popular among researchers and readers as the more traditional forms of local history.

Confusion occurs when the promoters of regional history appear totally to condemn the study of basic small-scale localities such as villages and towns, parishes and townships. Like it or not, such histories will continue to be written by both laymen and professionals — because such units were historically real, created their

---

[1] Marshall, *Tyranny of the Discrete*, p. 89.
[2] P. Clark & J. Hosking, *Population Estimates of English Small Towns, 1550-1851* (Leicester, 1993); M. Spufford, *Chippenham to the World: Microcosm to Macrocosm* (Roehampton Inst., 1995).
[3] A. Hassell Smith (ed.), *The Papers of Nathaniel Bacon of Stiffkey* (3 vols, 1979-90); Anne Mitson, 'The Significance of Kinship Networks in the 17th Century: South-West Nottinghamshire' in C. Phythian-Adams (ed.), *Societies, Cultures and Kinship, 1580-1850* (1993).
[4] For specific examples, see J. D. Marshall, 'Communities, Societies, Regions and Local History: Perceptions of Locality in High and Low Furness', *TLH*, 26, 1 (Feb. 1996), 36-47.

own administrative records, and can be studied manageably. Villages and towns were undeniably 'historical communities' which retained importance for many centuries.[1]   Indeed the writing of a parish history is an acknowledgement that a community of some kind still exists today. Everything possible should be done to ensure that these studies are critical and comparative, and that they always connect with the outside world. Today nobody really doubts 'that local studies should be set in the wider context of the neighbourhood'.[2] There are, after all, some good models to emulate. Where would English history now be without the classic studies of Wigston Magna, Myddle, Terling, Havering, Whickham and Camberwell? Newer examples bidding to become classics, most of them urban rather than rural, are still appearing regularly from places such as Stiffkey, Lutterworth, Retford, Wells and Carlisle.[3]   Admittedly these were all written by academic specialists, and most of them stop well short of the 19th century. However, none of them is in any sense final because they can be questioned, modified and even replaced; their great value lies in the stimulus which they give both to local studies *and* to national history, to professionals *and* part-timers.

Professional historians have shown an interest in local history since the late 19th century, but in the last two decades their influence and involvement have increased enormously. Nowadays, established academics and postgraduate students, trained in national history, frequently and deliberately choose to study local subjects and local sources in a 'top-down' sense. They realise that this approach opens up a vast quarry of evidence and human experience.[4] In a very real sense they are practising local history but of course would not dream of describing their work as such, warily and somewhat snobbishly preferring to use labels like 'social', 'economic', 'demographic', 'ecclesiastical', 'legal' and so on.[5] Nevertheless, I do not doubt that eventually a national historian of note will proclaim, 'We're all local historians now'. In the meantime, it is satisfying that the study of localities is increasingly seen as 'academically correct' — so long as the troublesome label of 'local history' can be avoided![6]

---

[1] W. R. Powell, 'Local History in Theory and Practice', *Bulletin of the Institute of Historical Research*, xxxi (1958), 44.

[2] D. Hey in *TLH*, 28, 2 (May 1998), 123.

[3] For a list of 'classic' local studies in print, see Further Reading on pp. 86-7.

[4] 'One obvious reason for the boom in local history is the rise of the PhD industry': J. S. Morrill, *Seventeenth Century Britain, 1603-1714* (1980).

[5] John Marshall has usefully described this work as 'locational' and 'instrumental' rather than 'local': *Tyranny of the Discrete*, p. 5.

[6] Some people are embarrassed by the word 'local' because it seems to suggest narrow-minded parochialism. Is therefore the very term Local History under threat from trendy new coinages like 'community history'? My guess is that it will survive and outlive most of its competitors, because it is inclusive and conveys a broad if imprecise meaning.

In practice such research is conducted on three main levels:

1. *Large numbers of places and local records are sampled to find detailed evidence for wide-ranging subjects.* Good examples, using mainly printed sources, are Eamon Duffy's work on traditional religion before and after the Reformation, and Ronald Hutton's survey of 'The Ritual Year'.[1]

2. *The emphasis is put on a natural region or administrative county.* In their studies of the Vale of Berkeley and Tudor Suffolk, David Rollison and Diarmaid MacCulloch had differing objectives: the first to show the effects of early industrialisation and the second to analyse the workings of county government.[2]

3. *A single rural or urban community is studied intensively, usually for a limited period.* Good examples are J. V. Beckett on the rural manor of Laxton in Notts., and Martha Carlin on the medieval suburb of Southwark.[3]

It is worth remembering that those who have the courage to call themselves local historians, have also produced work at the same three levels, but from a perspective which is more obviously 'bottom-up'. If the end-result is good history, does it really matter from which direction people come to the subject? In the meantime relations are improving in other ways. For instance, more research involving the co-operation of professionals and part-timers reduces the barriers between them, and helps to legitimise and democratise scholarship at a time when universities wrestle with chronic financial shortages (see below, p. 31-2).[4]

The personal relationship between local and other historians raises a deeper intellectual problem concerning the 'particular' and 'general'. In 1965, in defence of local history, W. G. Hoskins quoted William Blake's maxim that 'to generalize is to be an idiot; to particularize is the alone distinction of merit'. In so doing, he was no doubt showing his relish for the lives of ordinary people, for real 'flesh and blood' history.[5] However, the quotation could also be taken to imply that facts are more important than generalisations: our job, antiquarian rather than historical, is to enjoy the piling up of information without worrying about its broader significance. This seemed confirmed more recently when another distinguished historian, Patrick Collinson, complained that 'the difficulty with

---

[1] E. Duffy, *Stripping the Altars* (1992): R. Hutton, *The Rise and Fall of Merry England* (1994).

[2] D. Rollison, *The Local Origins of Modern Society: Gloucestershire, 1500-1800* (1992); D. MacCulloch, *Suffolk and the Tudors: Politics and Religion in an English County, 1500-1600* (1986). An early example of this approach is A. L. Rowse's *Tudor Cornwall* (1941), written 'to depict the process of the Reformation in microcosm, in the compact small area and society of my native Cornwall'. Rowse claimed that this work was an essay in 'total history', an attempt 'to integrate local and national history, to cross-fertilize each other'.

[3] J. V. Beckett, *A History of Laxton: England's Last Open-Field Village* (1989); M. Carlin, *Medieval Southwark* (1996).

[4] It is also encouraging that some distinguished academics, despite multiple commitments, find time to address local societies, and that ordinary local historians are increasingly acknowledged in the forewords of professional writers.

[5] Chris Lewis points out the irony that Hoskins undermined Blake's opinion 'with every word that he has written': *Particular Places*, p. 45.

local and regional history is that everywhere is different, so that the subject by its very nature courts particularism and resists treatment on a general or national scale'.[1] This remark in fact reveals both the problem and the answer.

Local history *is* full of fascinating 'particulars', probably more so than any other form of history except biography, and in the last resort every human community is inescapably unique. The more we know about local life, the more varied, intricate and complicated it becomes. But if we are to make sense of local history, we must acknowledge that in spite of the ultimate uniqueness of all places, 'some are less different than others'.[2] We must seek patterns of similarity and contrast, attempt broader judgements and generalisations, and not shrink from relating our work to models of human development produced by historians, anthropologists, social scientists or anyone else. Nor, conversely, must the national historian be afraid to face the 'particularism' of local history, which is always undermining and refining his broader generalisations. The purpose of comparison and generalisation is to establish what was 'normal' in the past, and what was unusual or even unique. That, as Margaret Spufford said many years ago, is the problem 'that... bedevils or should bedevil all local historians'.[3] If all this makes the job of the local historian more demanding, it nevertheless offers a further prize of immense worth.

A great virtue of local history is that it resists fragmentation and over-specialisation. At its best, unlike other branches of history, it remains wide-ranging, inclusive, integrating and interdisciplinary. To use a medical analogy, the local historian is more like a general practitioner than a consultant, prepared to show the connectedness of things and to follow where evidence leads. He is not inclined to divide his subject up into short arbitrary periods and small thematic specialisms or 'tunnels', a process which Keith Wrightson has lamented as intellectual 'enclosure'.[4] We all know that concepts like 'social man' and 'economic man' are unreal abstractions, and that our proper task is to reconstruct human lives as completely as possible, given the sources available. As local history becomes steadily more critical and comparative (not necessarily professional), one hopes that it will be seen as spearheading the fight against endless sub-division and over-specialisation, perhaps becoming 'one of the most promising and exciting growth-points in the discipline of history as a whole'.[5]

---

[1] Patrick Collinson, *The Birthpangs of Protestant England* (Macmillan, 1988), p. 49.

[2] Lewis, *Particular Places*, p. 35.

[3] M. Spufford, 'The Total History of Village Communities', *TLH*, 10, 8 (Nov. 1973), 400. Phythian-Adams put it differently by writing about 'that vital link between the particular and general which is so necessary for the academic advance of the discipline': Foreword to A. Everitt, *Continuity and Colonization* (1986), p. xiii.

[4] 'Increasingly, the social history of early modern England is being farmed in chronological, thematic and conceptual severalty': K. Wrightson, 'The Enclosure of English Social History' in A. Wilson (ed.), *Rethinking Social History* (Manchester UP, 1993), pp. 59-77. Similarly John Marshall devoted a whole chapter of his *Tyranny of the Discrete* to the fragmentation of academic history.

[5] Phythian-Adams (ed.), *Societies, Cultures and Kinship, 1580-1850* (1993), p. xii.

2. THE CHALLENGE OF WRITING

The most important works of history often seem to the general reader rather dull and
technical, while the popular successes usually merit the censure of the historian. It is
no easy task to be both interesting and accurate.
(A. J. P. Taylor, *Manchester Guardian*, 4 Dec. 1936)

This book is intended to help any who find themselves tempted (or expected) to
write history, but who for various reasons are held back by hesitations and doubts.
It is aimed, for example, at those who enjoy historical research but have never
committed their ideas to paper; and at others who, having written academic essays
and dissertations, wonder about putting that work into a more accessible published
form.[1] The message of these pages is simple. *If you feel tempted to write, accept the
challenge — but take the task very seriously.* In following this optimistic and encouraging
line, one naturally runs the risk of attracting criticism from all sides: the part-timer
or amateur can be easily deterred by advice which seems pedantic and over-demand-
ing, while the professional or specialist is easily annoyed by an approach which
seems populist and not sufficiently critical. However, my firm belief is that by
deliberately focusing on the details of research and writing, we can all derive more
satisfaction from the study of history and achieve higher personal standards. The
fact that this book, originally written in 1981, has had to be revised in 1998, convinces
me that more people than ever are anxious to write, and to write better. Behind this
growth are factors such as increased leisure (at least for some), longer retirement,
the boom in family history, and new educational and recreational opportunities.
Above all, we now seem less intimidated by the *thought* of writing, partly because of
the practical advantages offered by computers and desk-top publishing.

However, some would-be writers are undoubtedly confused by the fact that
published local history takes so many different forms. At one extreme are full-blown

---

[1] Local history may be the subject, solely or partially, of dissertations at various academic levels. It
features not only in those written for higher degrees (e.g. MPhil, PhD, etc), but also in those forming
part of many first-degree courses, and also within certain A-level syllabuses (for example, A.E.B. 673
and London E). This option will remain in new A-levels to be introduced in 2000.

books which obviously demand a major commitment of time and effort.[1] On the other hand a great deal of publishing is smaller in scale and appears as articles in national and local journals, chapters in edited collections and notes in newsletters. At the more popular end of the spectrum are collections of historical photographs, articles in newspapers and commercial magazines, guide-books, trails, pamphlets and leaflets. Beginners who lack experience and confidence in writing are probably best advised to start by attempting something which is limited and manageable. A few hours in a local-studies or university library will soon reveal the range of outlets available. In particular one will identify the journals, newsletters and bulletins which abound in all counties and regions, the balance of their contents, and what they require of writers submitting articles or notes.[2]

Faced with this range of outlets, beginners often ask: for whom are we writing, or for whom *should* we write? To some extent the answer depends on the medium they feel most comfortable with. An article for a specialised journal will be suitable for one kind of audience, while a parish history, a newspaper article or an historical trail will each be aimed at a different blend of readers. Yet the differences should be of degree only, not of kind: they concern the length and elaboration of the text, and the extent of technicalities such as footnotes and bibliographies. They should not involve changes in the actual *style* of writing which in its clarity, coherence and elegance should always be capable of appealing to the widest possible audience. In the stirring words of R. M. Robbins, 'the more people read a piece of published work, the better ... *The audience, or the readership, that we seek must be the largest that the subject can possibly be made to interest.*'[3] Furthermore, all kinds of written history should assume interest and intelligence on the part of readers, but not necessarily prior knowledge and experience. Finally, we need to be reminded of the pleasure and advantages of working at different levels: an individual writer does not have to restrict himself to one kind of publication. Some of our busiest and most engaged local historians write not only for their colleagues and peers (important though that is, mainly through established periodicals), but also seize every chance of communicating with the 'general public' through, for example, newspapers and local radio.

---

[1] Theses and dissertations are regarded as 'unpublished' because only a few copies are produced. It is obviously desirable that good studies of this sort be subsequently turned into published articles or books. Details of completed theses and dissertations can be found in journals such as *JORALS* and *Urban History*. The Institute of Historical Research of the University of London publishes annually *Historical Research for Higher Degrees in the United Kingdom* (listing completed theses and those in progress).
[2] This assumes that the local historian is a 'Lone Ranger', which is normally the case. However, the beginner may be lucky enough to find an attractive group project being run by an enterprising local society (see below, p. 31).
[3] *Antiquaries Jour.*, lxviii, pt 1 (1988), 3-4.

These quite rare individuals are the true visionaries of our subject, because they never forget their broader social and communal responsibilities.[1]

Nevertheless, the writing of history is not easy, particularly when one deliberately aims at a wide readership. The most obvious problem today is that good research is often divorced from good writing, and *vice versa*. On the one hand, many writers are unable (or unwilling) to communicate their thoughts with sufficient lucidity and directness. Consequently their readers have to read passages several times before getting the gist.[2] This failing can be found in all kinds of writing, but is very common in the work of professional academics. On the other hand, dedicated and loving work is frequently published with standards of research which are not rigorous and critical enough. This offence must be laid at the door, almost exclusively, of non-professional and part-time historians. The problem is best illustrated by looking at two short examples.

The first was written by a university teacher of some eminence. He was discussing an important problem which is familiar to all practising historians, the difficulty of using two or more documents which *may* be referring to the same historical individual:

> From this claim, if it stands, it follows that historical existence claims, historical predicate corroboration and the growth of historical knowledge in general, presuppose historical record linkage.

One can understand how an educated man may produce such foggy verbosity in a preliminary draft, but how could he in good conscience submit it for publication? And how could it be accepted by an editor and publisher, as this was? Are such inaccessible phrases deliberately adopted as a way of flaunting esoteric learning? Or even as a way of deterring *hoi polloi*? Writing of this kind surely indicates that something is wrong not only with our standards of general education, but also with the specific way in which academics are trained (or not trained) to turn their thoughts into writing.[3] Of course, the complexities of history inevitably demand effort of both writer and reader, but the historian's use of language should not be allowed to compound the difficulties.

---

[1] Two examples. Carl Chinn is an authority on the history of modern Birmingham; his publications include studies of urban poverty, council housing, bookmaking and the local impact of World War II. He broadcasts on local radio and masterminds a 32-page monthly supplement to a local newpaper called the 'Old Brum Mag' — of which about 10,000 copies are regularly distributed. In the very different environment of rural north Devon, Peter Christie teaches history for the Open University and in an FE College. He is a town and district councillor, who was mayor of Bideford in 1985, and has written hundreds of short popular articles on local and family history for two local newspapers.

[2] It could be argued that we have returned to the pompous and convoluted prose of Victorian times. Certainly some of the most turgid examples of local literature are parish histories written by 19th-century clergy.

[3] As editor of *The Local Historian* for eight years, I soon got used to receiving articles from academics which contained frequent stylistic and grammatical failures, as well as elementary spelling mistakes.

The second example is utterly different in flavour, and was written by an enthusiastic and industrious individual who wanted to contribute to the history of her own village:

> It seemed such a pity to have all these bits and pieces lying about, so I decided to put them in chronological order.

This sad apology reminds us of the plight of many aspiring local historians. The growing popularity of the subject means that an ever-increasing number of people amass information but unfortunately make little creative use of it. They assume that readers only want to be diverted by quaint facts and colourful anecdotes, arranged in chronological order. Some of them (certainly not all) have genuine critical and literary ability, but have never been sufficiently helped to write, or to face the challenge of evidence and academic debate. It is now easier than ever before to be overwhelmed and buried by the information one finds, and therefore to regard the mechanical accumulation of information as *the* purpose of history.

The danger, therefore, is that writers of history are torn between two false ideals: on the one hand, academic incomprehensibility and on the other, undemanding readability. The situation is made worse by those publishers who abuse the popular appeal of the subject by commissioning inadequate books from ill-prepared authors, or who allow poorly written work to pass. Editors of some journals must also accept their share of blame.[1] In every British region we see the publication of badly prepared and poorly written history, which in turn makes it more difficult for others to teach the subject effectively. Although professionals regularly castigate amateur historians for their antiquarianism and myopia, the latter are surprisingly reluctant to criticise professionals for their frequent abuse of language. In fact, both faults are serious and fundamental. And another danger now looms, for the computing revolution in history threatens to create a new kind of antiquarianism with its own special jargon and obtuseness of language.

But does this range of written standards matter greatly when fine works of local history are published quite often? My answer is that it does matter, for a variety of reasons. First, highly variable standards of writing condemn local history in the eyes of too many people. This is one reason why, for example, many academics dismiss local history as antiquarian and 'parochial'. Secondly, I do not believe that such standards are inevitable for all time and can never be raised. Local history need not be written obscurely or uncritically — especially if the virtues of structured research and conscientious writing are taught together. The third and last reason is the most important. Because local history is about ordinary, everyday life, and

---

[1] Authors, quite naturally, have a possessive attitude to their own prose, but they can react very differently to alterations proposed by editors. Some refuse to acknowledge their own weaknesses and resent the interference, while others, equally uncritically, accept every suggestion with a cheerful lack of concern.

therefore has an educational and social importance, we who profess the subject should value clear, well-researched writing particularly highly. We should feel no shame in making our work available to the largest possible readership.

Indeed ours is a very special branch of history which interests large numbers of people, and gives rise to a voluminous literature which librarians and booksellers, in their embarrassment, usually classify as 'English Topography' or 'Local Interest'.[1] *No other subject in the academic spectrum can so easily bridge the gulf between the specialist and man-in-the-street.* In fact it frequently annihilates that gulf because the 'expert' turns out to have had no special training, and the layman is often able to contribute special skills and knowledge of his own. Could anything be more beneficial in an age when the study of history constantly fragments?

---

[1] Biography and military history are also very popular. However, if we include all forms of published local history (e.g. commercial 'county' magazines, church guides, parish magazines, local newspapers, etc.), it is probably the most widely read.

RESEARCH

1.   CHOOSE SUBJECT to investigate (adjusting three dimensions of theme, place & period); be prepared to revise as work proceeds.

2.   FIND SOURCES & EVIDENCE

| Books and articles
references
more reading | Primary documents
transcribing
abstracts, extracts | Oral evidence
transcribing | Physical evidence
fieldwork
maps |

3.   AMASS and CONTROL INFORMATION:
       references, notes, transcripts, facsimiles, etc. stored in files, card-indexes, databases, etc.

4.   ANALYSE EVIDENCE, both words and numbers, by using carefully designed forms, spreadsheets, etc., and thereby create new evidence and generalisations.

5.   RE-READ and SORT all evidence BEFORE WRITING; reject that which is not essential.

6.   QUESTION SOURCES, to weigh their relative strengths and weaknesses.

7.   SYNTHESISE and INTERPRET: survey evidence in the light of other historians' work (secondary sources), and think out the historical argument to be presented. This process should have begun at the start, but climaxes here as one prepares to write.

> Constantly question and compare the primary and secondary evidence as it accumulates.
>
> Continue to look for new evidence and new comparative studies.
>
> Talk to other historians.

WRITING

8.   WRITE OUTLINE OF TEXT, in skeletal form, establishing order of presentation (chapters, sub-headings, etc.) and main twists and turns of argument.

9.   WRITE FIRST DRAFT: keep the prose flowing by writing quickly; amendments, improvements and references can be added later.

10.   RE-DRAFT as many times as necessary; this often involves substantial alteration. Seek the criticism of others.

11.   PUBLISH: deal with editors, printers, publishers, or be your own desk-top publisher.

Fig. 1   Processes of Research and Writing: A Summary

3. CHOOSING A SUBJECT

One of the most important tasks facing the would-be writer is so elementary that it is often overlooked. He or she must carefully define a subject for research. This choice is influenced by a host of factors, personal and historical, such as our existing knowledge, our educational and family background, the aspects of life which interest us most, and of course the availability of sources.[1] With a clear and measured objective, however large or small, we can concentrate attention more effectively and recognise the potential and relevance of evidence as it is found. Otherwise it is easy to waste time, sometimes a lifetime, vaguely enjoying the collection of snippets of information, but not thinking about their relative value in a defined project. It should also be recognised that subjects may have to be re-defined or at least modified, as new evidence becomes known. Some topics lead to the discovery of abundant sources, in which case the terms of reference may have to be reduced; conversely other topics reveal an embarrassing lack of sources, and therefore the coverage may have to be widened.[2]

The main stimulus in choosing a subject is *not* a full appreciation of the relevant sources. We cannot possibly know all the evidence before we start, though we hope to know some of it. *The unavoidable starting-point must be a genuine interest in some aspect of human life which is arguably significant.* This means that we must probe our own motives with care, and ask why are we attracted to a particular slice of history. Is it because it seems romantic or quaint, or because an interesting document or piece of landscape took our fancy? Is there a danger that our fascination with bits of evidence and pleasant stories will divert us from the main task of creating our own

---

[1] If one is working with others, perhaps as members of an adult class or of a local society, the definition of a project depends heavily on the dynamics and organisation of the group, and also on its leadership. However, 'Research Classes' which were fashionable in the 1960s and '70s have waned in numbers. In the 1990s, because of the proliferation of qualifications in Local History, most new research in adult education is done by individuals working on their own but under supervision. It may be, however, that the new insistence on accreditation will stimulate a revival of group research, with the emphasis on primary sources.

[2] But these are not invariable rules. A small body of evidence can be used, with ingenuity, to tell a fascinating human story. For example, Eileen Power's famous essay on 'Thomas Paycocke of Coggeshall' in Essex, was based on no more than three very different sources, his will, house and memorial brass: *Medieval People* (1924).

vision of the past? Of course, in any historical project we must have sources, and the discovery of a cache of documents has frequently led to distinguished writing. But evidence is there to be used and therefore transformed into original, humane history.

In practice our interest often focuses on a subject, a problem, an area of uncertainty, or a body of evidence which nobody has tackled before. We try, in other words, to find an historical space which we can claim as our own. Even there, we will always find points of contact with what other historians have already done and written. In that sense, *no piece of research is ever divorced from existing knowledge.*[1] *Woe betide the historian who forgets this, and writes as if he were in a vacuum.* Looked at more realistically, therefore, our wish may be to fill certain gaps in the record, or to show our dissatisfaction with the existing state of knowledge, and thus contribute to a current debate or controversy.[2]

On narrowing down the options, we soon find that three dimensions have to be adjusted: THEME, TIME and PLACE. In order to satisfy ourselves and our evidence, we must decide on a particular theme of human history, in a particular area, over a certain length of time. Of course the number of possible variations is infinite, and we can already see an amazing plurality of approaches. This is why local history shades imperceptibly into many other forms of history, as can be seen on the shelves of any good library, and why we should never waste time arguing that local history is an independent discipline. The three dimensions mentioned above are worth discussing individually. Quite deliberately we shall begin with 'theme' — even though for most local historians the choice of 'place' comes first and is totally unnegotiable!

THEME

It is helpful to think of the study of local history as divided into seven broadly distinct yet overlapping areas of interest. Starting with the most basic and working towards the more personal, they are:

- **landscape history** (or **topography**)
  - soils, relief, archaeology, settlement, field-systems, town plans, etc.
- **population history** (or **demography**)
  - rise & fall of population; crises; family & kin; mobility & stability
- **economic history**
  - property & landholding; agriculture, commerce, industry & transport; prices & wages; standards of living
- **social history**
  - wealth & poverty, social status, groups & classes, welfare & charity

[1] Or, as Keith Wrightson put it, 'No historian writes a book alone': *English Society, 1580-1680* (1982), p. 9.
[2] Historians are by nature argumentative people, for ever promoting their own interpretations and heroes, and looking critically at those of their colleagues.

- **political history**
  - power, control, law & order; secular & ecclesiastical administration; governing élites
- **cultural history**
  - music, drama and art; leisure, entertainment & sport; folk-memory, literacy & education, etc.
- **intellectual history**
  - ideas, values & beliefs (communal, inherited or personal); philosophies & religious creeds.[1]

Writers of traditional parish and county histories often touched on all these areas in a summary way, and a few brave souls still attempt the same broad-brush approach. Then and now, any historians wishing to depict whole communities, in however brief a form, have to consider all seven of these levels, and the ways in which they inevitably overlap and interact.

Nevertheless, most present-day researchers have more limited objectives; they do not necessarily agree with each others' priorities or show an equal interest in all facets of the past. They tend to concentrate on particular topics which excite them and for which sufficient evidence can be found. For example someone interested in religion may concentrate on protestant nonconformity, or on an individual sect like Primitive Methodism, or even on the fortunes of a single chapel. Another possibility is to write about a particular source, particularly a new or underused one, to debate its potentialities and limitations. Some writers choose subjects because they appear to have been of outstanding importance at a particular period. Like all good historians, they are primarily driven by the desire to answer certain pressing questions rather than simply to use a particular body of evidence. This means that themes may be chosen for which the evidence is relatively meagre or difficult to interpret: for example the recreational life of ordinary people, the nature of popular religious beliefs, or the effectiveness of education.

The range of choice faced by local historians has expanded greatly in the past fifty years, as virtually every aspect of life has come under investigation and an ever widening number of sources has been exploited. If a would-be researcher is uncertain about where to start, a trawl through journals in the last ten years will soon reveal current trends and areas of debate. For example, today's fashionable topics include medicine, charity, ethnic minorities, the role of women, entertainment and sport, crime and policing. Many of the subjects now chosen by local historians are already

---

[1] One can argue that these seven subject-areas have an *ascending* order of human significance, because they range from fundamentals such as settlement patterns and demographic trends to abstract and personal considerations such as educational standards and religious belief. This does not mean that the study of, say, landscape history is any less critical or demanding than religious history.

academic specialisations in their own right, with their own experts, textbooks, societies and journals. This offers the chance of acquiring important background information, and of reading useful comparative studies. Part-timers now tend to follow the lead of professionals in wanting to tackle subjects which are both manageable and of current interest. After all, some of the most active students of local history have taken up the subject in retirement, and they are well aware that time has its limits.

However, a great danger lies in too much specialisation. Academic divisions do not reflect the past itself, but are caused by professional emphasis on particular themes or kinds of evidence; they are what J. H. Hexter called 'tunnel history'.[1] *The local historian's task, admittedly within narrower geographical limits, is to provide as broad and synoptic a view of the past as he can.* In these days of ever-increasing specialisation and fragmentation, he puts the emphasis on integration and synthesis (see above, p. 11). Certainly he will draw on the work of specialists, read their journals and even contribute to them, but his concern with the life of the whole community usually gives him a more integrative and reconciling role. For example, the study of an agricultural estate in the 18th century may lead to a discussion of local population trends, the variable distribution of wealth, the exercise of political power, the control of religious denominations, and the changing tastes of élites. Whatever the chosen topic, we as local historians want to relate it to the life of the wider community in a way which does not attract the average specialist working in his 'tunnel'.

To develop the subject more deeply, a small number of professional writers have swum against the tide and attempted to write 'total history'. This is not the approach adopted in the traditional parish or town history, which usually ranges over long periods in a summary and eclectic way. On the contrary it is an attempt to show how a community worked *as a whole*, and how its constituent parts interwove in the complex texture of local life. The aim, however impossible it sounds (and in the last resort it *is* impossible), is to study 'life … in its entirety'.[2] In practice such an ambitious task can only be attempted for relatively short periods. An early example written in 1974 was Margaret Spufford's *Contrasting Communities*, in which she aimed at the total history of three parishes during the Tudor and Stuart period. The increase of breadth is clear enough, though it must be said that some aspects of life, for example the recreational dimension, are still missing. Alan Macfarlane later stressed the value of linking scattered references to as many individuals as possible within a given community. For this purpose he saw twelve categories of documents as central, including parish registers, wills and court rolls.[3] Although that sounded 'total'

---

[1] J. H. Hexter, *Reappraisals in History* (1961), pp. 194-5.
[2] M. Spufford, 'The Total History of Village Communities', *TLH*, 10, 8 (1973), 398.
[3] A. Macfarlane, *Reconstructing Historical Communities* (1977), pp. 42-80.

enough, Barry Stapleton showed that, after laboriously reconstituting families from parish registers, one can still weave in personal information from over seventy other kinds of record.[1]

Not surprisingly, the quest for total history has been only a partial success. Striving to cover every possible dimension of local life can become a great mental burden, almost an obsession, and may lead to a serious loss of focus. And even with the help of powerful computers, this broad and detailed approach does not seem to have revolutionised the *writing* of history. Even if we achieve a thematic coverage which is close to 'total', our final interpretations are still generalising and therefore selective. Although the objective of 'total history' is now mentioned less often than in the 1970s, it has certainly had a good effect in encouraging local historians to investigate the past more holistically. Perhaps it is best regarded, not so much as an achievable gaol, but as a worthwhile approach and attitude of mind.

As has already been said, most of today's local historians wisely choose to work on quite limited topics which seem manageable in the time available. Even so, they usually complain that research turns out to be more complex and time-consuming than at first appeared, and that it has the habit of expanding in unexpected directions! An astonishing variety of themes can be found in contemporary journals and other publications. For instance, during the last ten years writers of articles in *The Local Historian* have tackled subjects as diverse as the work of a country doctor, pawn-broking in Leicester, public parks in Weston-super-Mare, and the naming of streets in the East End of London. The current craze for publishing historical photographs, particularly early postcards, demands captions of a high standard — much higher, in fact, than is normally achieved. Another opportunity lies in the writing of guide-books and 'trails'. A high proportion of existing guides to churches are inadequate and ought to be replaced, and many places of worship have no guide at all; similar opportunities beckon at many other accessible buildings and archaeological sites.[2] Well-planned trails help the general public to explore whole streets, districts and countrysides, not only drawing attention to physical features which are often over-looked, but putting them into proper historical context. If we are to escape from the present over-concentration on major monuments — and neglect of the less obvious and more vulnerable visual history which is always and everywhere around us — many more such aids will have to be written (and kept up-to-date) for residents and

---

[1] B. Stapleton, 'Sources for the Demographic Study of a Local Community from the 16th to the mid-19th Century', *JORALS*, vol.4, no.2 (1984), 1-26.

[2] D. Dymond, *Writing a Church Guide* (Church Information Office, 1980). The Cheshire Churches Project has published guides for both adults and children, a trail for Chester and a general book; it has also provided interpretative panels outside churches. The Redundant Churches Fund (now the Churches Conservation Trust) has been publishing useful guides since the 1970s.

visitors alike. Fortunately, this kind of work may now receive the active encouragement and co-operation of local authorities and amenity societies.[1]

PLACE

For generations the majority of local historians have chosen, more by instinct than reason, to study the place in which they live or were born. And they have normally assumed that 'place' equals 'community'. This is not surprising because one's home district is part of one's life: its houses, its hidden corners, the church or chapel which stand for something more than the earthbound, sad but evocative tombstones, the fields and their names, the river or canal which was so magnetic in childhood, the offices and factories which symbolise work and routine — all these represent the lives of countless people who have lived, worked and died there. The place itself is primary evidence of human endeavour, which needs interpretation as much as any document, and which for many of us was the original spur to our historical imaginations. Therefore, many of us prefer to write about the places and communities which we know, feel part of, and love. At the same time we may have a consciously social purpose, a desire to help foster a sense of local identity and pride. W. J. Fishman's remarkable book on the East End of London has been described as combining 'family loyalty, childhood and adolescent memory and tenderness', to the extent that it 'helps to warm the human spirit'.[2] Nobody should be ashamed of these motives, although they court dangers and some commentators will condemn us for being too sentimental, too desperate in our search for a stable and comfortable world that never was.

Any local or regional study which does not convey a clear sense of place is stunted. An acclaimed history of an Essex parish published in 1979 gave fascinating insight into the polarisation of rural society in the early 17th century, but read as if the writers had never been there. A map of 1597 was not reproduced, and the topography of the traditional village and farming landscape, which is well preserved, was barely mentioned.[3] The physical setting of a local society is not only part of its uniqueness, but is important historical evidence in itself. Moreover, it can easily be forgotten that 'place' also incorporates the more dynamic notion of 'space'. How did the distances which former generations encountered in their working and social lives

---

[1] Good examples are leaflets under the general title of 'Stepping Out', produced by North Kesteven District Council with support from the Lincolnshire County Council and the Countryside Commission. They describe rural walks which have been physically improved and waymarked. A series of larger booklets, describing walks around towns, has been published by the Suffolk Preservation Society, sometimes in association with a more local amenity society.

[2] Richard Cobb's foreword in W. J. Fishman, *East End, 1888* (1988). Another good example is John Bestall's determination that his native Chesterfield should have a worthy history; so far three volumes of a projected five have appeared.

[3] K. Wrightson & D. Levine, *Poverty and Piety in an English Village: Terling, 1525-1700* (Academic Press, 1979 and 1995).

affect their view of themselves, and of the outside world?[1] How did the mental maps and horizons of different social groups change over time? And how do we as historians shed modern values and reconstruct the spatial perceptions of earlier generations? Although many historical specialists overlook the importance of place and space, the local historian can never afford to do so. By a combination of maps, illustrations and particularly words, he must give the reader a coherent impression of the landscape or townscape, and patterns of communication, which contained and influenced his human story.

Another good reason for studying a particular place-cum-community is that it is well documented, either in a general sense or by having a single outstanding source. David Hey wrote his fascinating account of Myddle in Shropshire not because he lived there, but because it offered one of the most remarkable sources known to English historians — a contemporary account of its inhabitants by a 17th-century resident called Richard Gough.[2] Of course, Gough's description which is based on direct experience and memory, is quite exceptional. In general we are looking for sources which are relevant to a chosen topic, and sufficiently organised in layout to allow proper analysis. But, with any choice of subject, we are at the mercy of our sources — good, bad and indifferent — and have to make the best of them.

Sadly, many local historians miss good opportunities because they obstinately refuse to sample larger areas. Parishes within a few miles of each other will show massive variations in the quantity and quality of their records, and a few outstandingly rich sources will always cry out for attention. Similarly each individual parish will have its own strengths and weaknesses. In the rural corner of Suffolk in which I lived for twenty years, within four contiguous parishes, Stanton has an unusually rich collection of medieval charters, Walsham-le-Willows has exceptional manorial surveys and poor-law records, Bardwell has the accounts of a late-medieval guild and a good town-book, and Stowlangtoft has the autobiography and correspondence of a 17th-century squire who was also a national figure. Their records from the 18th to 20th centuries are equally patchy: for example Stowlangtoft has very few records for the 19th century, but Bardwell has a superb parish magazine (starting in 1892) which is virtually a village newspaper. *The point is that simply to investigate the life of a single parish, one needs to browse among the resources of a whole district. Although the local historian rightly acknowledges the centuries-old significance of parish boundaries, he must never regard them as impenetrable barriers.* Administrative boundaries never

---

[1] In a WEA Summer School I once received a remarkable autobiographical essay from an elderly woman, a gamekeeper's daughter, who had been brought up before World War I in a remote Breckland hamlet. The town of Bury St Edmunds, only six miles away, was rarely visited by the family: to the children it therefore acquired a glamorous and somewhat magical significance, like some distant Shangri-La.

[2] D. G. Hey, *An English Rural Community: Myddle under the Tudors and Stuarts* (1974); David Hey (ed.), *Richard Gough, The History of Myddle* (1981).

prevented the movement of people and influences in the past, and they should not stunt anyone's vision in the present (Fig.2, p. 26).

In the last generation, a growing number of historians has chosen to study *groups* of parish communities. This broader approach has been usefully dubbed 'comparative local history' because it brings into sharper focus the common inheritance *and* the uniqueness of such places — two major objectives in local research.[1] Thus Margaret Spufford in her *Contrasting Communities* worked on three widely-spaced Cambridgeshire parishes which she saw as representative of different sub-regions within the county. Her book appeared almost simultaneously with Jack Ravensdale's *Liable to Floods* which also dealt with three Cambridgeshire parishes, but this time adjacent ones at the southern end of the Fens.[2] The first study concentrated on human issues such as population, social structure and religion, while the second was primarily concerned with 'village landscape'. Another instructive example is Victor Skipp's work on five adjacent parishes in the Forest of Arden, which he regarded as 'a small piece of England in a test-tube'.[3]

In the search for larger territories suitable for study, a few writers have opted for historic administrative districts within counties, whether secular or ecclesiastical. For instance, H. E. Hallam studied the medieval reclamation of fenland in Elloe, a 'wapentake' of south Lincolnshire, while David Hey has illuminated the social and industrial history of an early ecclesiastical unit (incorporating Sheffield) called Hallamshire.[4] More frequently the preferred unit of study has been a geological-cum-geographical area with its own distinctive natural and man-made countryside (in other words a *pays*) such as the Weald of Kent, the Lake District, the Forest of Dean or the Yorkshire Wolds. Alan Everitt designated eight main types of *pays* ranging from fellsides to coastal marshes, and has argued that they influenced not just the character of human settlement and farming but even cultural and religious behaviour.[5]

An even more common choice for study, with a long pedigree stretching back for centuries, is the county or shire. Older county histories such as Sir William Dugdale's *Warwickshire* (1656) or John Bridges' *Northamptonshire* (1791) were almost entirely concerned with landowning families, their estates, manors, country houses, heraldry and genealogy, and with the clergy and their churches.[6] Modern county histories

---

[1] A. Rogers in *LHM*, 68 (July/Aug. 1998), 18.
[2] M. Spufford, *Contrasting Communities: English Villagers in the 16th and 17th Centuries* (1974); J. R. Ravensdale, *Liable to Floods: Village Landscape on the Edge of the Fens, AD 450-1850* (1974).
[3] V. Skipp, *Crisis and Development: An Ecological Case Study of the Forest of Arden, 1570-1674* (CUP, 1978), p. 5
[4] H. E. Hallam, *New Lands of Elloe* (1954); D. Hey, *The Fiery Blades of Hallamshire: Sheffield and its Neighbourhood, 1660-1740* (Leicester UP, 1991).
[5] A. Everitt, 'Country, County and Town: Patterns of Regional Evolution in England', *Trans. Royal Historical Soc.*, 5th series, 29 (1979), 84-5.
[6] C. R. J. Currie & C. P. Lewis (eds), *English County Histories: A Guide* (1994).

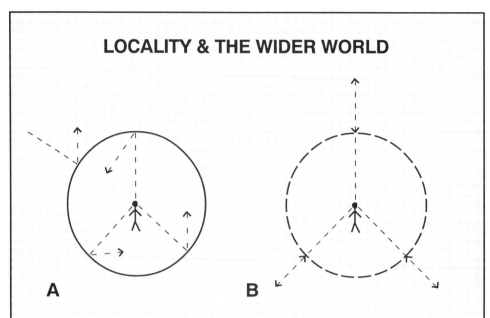

LOCALITY & THE WIDER WORLD

A

B

This diagram attempts to illustrate a crucial choice faced by the local historian who prefers to work on a basic administrative unit such as a parish or township. Standing, as it were, in the centre of his chosen place, he can regard the boundary in one of two ways: as an impenetrable physical and mental barrier, a sort of Berlin Wall (A); or as porous in both directions (B). The first approach is blinkered and will certainly not reveal the true significance of local life. The second will give much better shape and meaning to research and writing, because it acknowledges that every community contributes to the life of other broader groupings and in turn is affected by them. These vital and illuminating connections with the wider world can take many different forms, but will be of three main kinds which are given here in order of (arguably) ascending importance:

Administrative & Legal	Geographical & Economic	Personal & Cultural
hundred, wapentake, deanery	hinterland of town	kinship network
archdeaconry, diocese	landed estate	social contacts
Quarter Sessions district	working zone	religious bonds
Poor Law union	farming region	cultural links
shire	industrial region	shared dialect
nation	'province'	mental maps

Fig. 2   Locality and The Wider World

are broader in scope and are, apart from the parochially-based *VCH*, of three main types. Some are 'popular' summaries covering huge swathes of time, from prehistory to the 20th century, like the Darwen series which devotes one slim volume to each county. Of a more substantial kind are detailed surveys like the twelve-volumed *History of Lincolnshire* which deals separately, for example, with prehistory, the medieval church and the 20th century.[1] Most specialised of all are single volumes dealing with specific themes such as early settlement and land-division, the role of the magistracy, and the upper-crust 'county community' around the time of the Civil Wars.[2] For certain topics, therefore, the county may be an appropriate unit of study, but in other contexts its choice seems arbitrary and swayed more by archival than historical considerations.[3]

For those with primarily rural interests, urban history now appears to have pulled away from other forms of local history. As David Marcombe has ably demonstrated, even a small market town like Retford (Notts.) is a much more complicated human organism than a rural parish.[4] To tackle a county town or a major industrial centre is an even greater enterprise, which may call for a shorter chronology or for concentration on fewer aspects of local life. On the other hand, Mary Prior shows that it may be worth studying distinctive *parts* of major towns, even individual streets, in the quest for human diversity.[5] One obviously under-explored aspect of urban history is the internal division of British towns — whether socially, ethnically, economically or by religion. How far did a parish, ward or other internal entity resemble the 'contrada' of Italian cities, generating fierce loyalty, ceremonial rivalry and even armed strife?[6]

Yet in spite of increasing specialisation, historians are fast coming to realise that urban and rural history should *never* be divorced. Every town, regardless of size or the length of its history, has around it a rural 'hinterland', an area of two-way economic and social influence which shows subtle and often unpredictable variations

---

[1] With one interesting exception, the volumes of 'The History of Lincolnshire' were each written by one individual. The final volume on the 20th century involved twelve contributors: D. R. Mills (ed.), *Twentieth Century Lincolnshire* (1989).

[2] A. Everitt, *Continuity and Colonization: The Evolution of Kentish Settlement* (1986); J. Blair, *Early Medieval Surrey* (1991); A. Hassell Smith, *County and Court: Government and Politics in Norfolk, 1558-1603* (1987); A. Hughes, *Politics, Society and Civil War in Warwickshire, 1620-60* (1987). Another good example of the convenient scale of county history (yet having much wider significance) is David Hall's study of *The Open Fields of Northamptonshire* (Northants Record Soc., 38, 1995).

[3] In recent years two new kinds of published history have used county boundaries as a convenience, though their subjects largely override and ignore them! They are the historical atlas which presents and explains large numbers of distribution maps, and collections of aerial photographs which, with captions, interpret local landscapes and townscapes. Another reason for choosing a county scale has to do with marketing: local people are more likely to buy a study of 'Borsetshire' than one of the 'West Midlands'.

[4] D. Marcombe, *English Small Town Life: Retford, 1520-1642* (1993).

[5] Mary Prior, *Fisher Row: Fishermen, Bargemen and Canal Boatmen in Oxford, 1500-1900* (Oxford, 1982).

[6] A classic study of strife within a town is E. le R. Ladurie, *Carnival in Romans: A People's Uprising at Romans, 1579-1580* (Penguin Books, 1981).

over distance and time. This outer territory is an indispensable part of urban history, as demonstrated in John Goodacre's work on the market town of Lutterworth (Leics.) and in Maryanne Kowaleski's assessment of the region around medieval Exeter.[1] Conversely, rural and agricultural historians must always acknowledge the influence of local towns, large and small, dominant and modest, growing and failing — because a single village could simultaneously feel the pull of several towns of different rank. In other words, villages and towns do not inhabit different universes: they have always had a symbiotic and dynamic relationship which offers a fascinating challenge to all historians.

Finally, we must not forget the long-running debate on 'regional history' (see above, pp. 8-9). Faced with the tendency for academic history to fragment, and for much local history to focus on the single 'discrete' community, a number of professionals have argued for the identification of historical regions larger than the parish, manor or township.[2] They have postulated 'neighbourhoods' and 'societies' which may extend over six to ten miles, and even of large 'provinces' which could incorporate several counties.[3] Such territories, it is suggested, reflect and reveal human affiliations more accurately than purely administrative units or geographical zones. They are human groupings which had, at particular periods of the past, similar characteristics — whether social, economic, political, religious, or a combination of any of these. For instance, they may be traceable by marital or commercial links, the average size of farms, the prevalence of certain industrial occupations, religious affiliations, or even by rates of crime and bastardy. Some of these broader territories are mental concepts more than anything else, as they depend on the experience and contacts of groups and well-documented individuals.[4]

Historical regions can be of very different sizes in both area and population; they may also have been short-lived, and could indeed overlap. Some proponents of regional history maintain that one should *start* by trying to identify such wider groupings, however difficult the task; it has even been suggested that a larger area might be chosen *arbitrarily* in the hope that genuine affiliations will later emerge.[5] At a later stage, it is argued, one will be in a better position to understand the character of constituent towns and villages. Debates of this kind undoubtedly make us think much more about the factors which united and divided previous generations, who were capable

---

[1] J. Goodacre, *The Transformation of a Peasant Economy: Townspeople and Villagers in the Lutterworth Area, 1500-1700* (1994); M. Kowaleski, *Local Markets and Regional Trade in Medieval Exeter* (1996).
[2] The main vehicle is the Conference of Regional and Local Historians, which supports the *Journal of Regional and Local Studies* (*JORALS*).
[3] See C. Phythian-Adams, *Re-thinking English Local History* (Leicester UP, 1987); 'Introduction: An Agenda for English Local History' in Phythian-Adams (ed.), *Societies, Cultures and Kinship, 1580-1850* (Leicester UP, 1993).
[4] J. D. Marshall, 'Communities, Societies, Regions and Local History: Perceptions of Locality in High and Low Furness', *TLH*, 26, 1 (Feb. 1996), 36-47.
[5] Phythian-Adams, *Re-thinking English Local History*, p. 43; Marshall, *Tyranny of the Discrete*, pp. 83-4.

of viewing the same locality differently over time. Such awareness can actually lead in opposite directions: towards the definition of groups *larger* than the parish or town, which is the main objective of Regional History, and towards the recognition of important human associations and divisions *within* and *across* individual parishes.

TIME

The traditional kind of parish history had a very broad chronological canvas. It usually brought the story down to the 19th century, or to the 'present day', but the starting point varied greatly. It could be 1086 because of the towering importance of Domesday Book, or the 5th to 7th centuries AD when Anglo-Saxon immigrants supposedly moved into an abandoned wilderness, or even deep in prehistory on the basis of a few known artefacts or sites. This kind of 'general' history has always been a difficult undertaking. Now it is even more difficult because of the volume of new research and the staggering proliferation of sources and techniques. For example it would be very unwise for a modern writer to ignore recent archaeological research into the origins of villages, scattered settlements, market towns and field-systems.[1] In spite of the difficulties, a significant number of individuals are still brave enough to attempt local history from A to Z and some, it must be admitted, produce books which are instructive and stimulating.[2]

A parish or town history need not always be a fat tome like Sir Matthew Nathan's *West Coker* with its 521 pages;[3] it may be a relatively slight volume or simply a pamphlet. The shorter the treatment, the greater the selectivity and judgement which the local historian has to exercise. He is forced to identify the most significant aspects of the local past. For example, the historian of a Fen-Breckland parish in East Anglia had the courage to say that the three main events in its history were the drainage of the fen in the 17th century, parliamentary enclosure in the early 19th century, and rapid expansion and suburbanisation since World War II.[4] Whether or not he is right, this is the kind of judgement and debate which local history should always contain. *Incidentally, it would be helpful if every local historical society set about the task of discussing, and attempting to identify, the outstanding themes of its area's history, but this happens only rarely.*

Because of the increasing sophistication of research and the sheer number of sources now available, many of today's local historians deliberately work within

---

[1] In this connection the most important journals to consult are *Medieval Archaeology, Landscape History* and the *Annual Report of the Medieval Settlement Research Group.*

[2] For example, M. K. Ashby, *The Changing English Village, 1066-1914* [Bledington, Glos.] (Roundwood Press, 1974); J. Chandler, *Endless Street: A History of Salisbury and its People* (Hobnob Press, 1983); N. Cooper, *Aynho: A Northamptonshire Village* (Leopard's Head Press, 1984); M. & F. Heywood & B. Jennings, *A History of Todmorden* (Smith Settle, 1996).

[3] Sir Matthew Nathan, *The Annals of West Coker* [Somerset] (CUP, 1957).

[4] In the 1960s-70s J. T. Munday, one of a dying breed of scholar-parsons, wrote and published a large number of pamphlets on the parishes of Eriswell and Lakenheath (Suffolk).

narrow chronological limits. They are not tempted by the full span of history, and they have abandoned the old temporal straitjackets of centuries, dynasties and reigns. Like other specialists they find it more satisfying to seek out relatively limited and 'short' topics: drawing out their full historical significance, discussing both their origins and consequences, and putting them into wider context. Within the last ten years, for example, articles have been published on such subjects as re-pewing a church in 1606, a riot over bridge-tolls in 1793, and a by-election in 1902.[1] *Other historians would undoubtedly contribute more to knowledge and keep in better touch with specialists if they attempted a less ambitious and more manageable chronology.* However, we should not go too far in squeezing our chronological perspectives: another of the distinguishing strengths of local history is a willingness to survey periods longer than those commonly used by other historians, and to make major comparisons over time.[2]

Finally, while on the subject of time, let us remember the value of recording the present for future generations. No better examples exist than the three multi-volumed *Statistical Accounts of Scotland* published in 1791-9, 1845 and 1951-92, which are all contemporary descriptions of life at local level (see sample in Appendix 2, p. 95). The need for work of this kind increases with the passage of time. At the beginning of the 21st century our society produces vast quantities of paper, film and tape, but it also destroys evidence on an unprecedented scale. Discussions on the telephone leave no trace; messages by 'fax' and e-mail are usually trashed; the art of letter-writing is fast dying; and today's local newspapers are no more than juvenile comics when compared to their solid predecessors of the 19th century. *Many aspects of contemporary local life will have no record unless we make it now — in both oral and documentary forms.* We may not be able to create a full and balanced picture of our own times, because we are too closely involved, but at least we can attempt the first historical account of recent and contemporary events. Why should local historians not grasp the opportunity of writing about the miners' strike of 1984-5, the 'troubles' in Northern Ireland, or the 'gentrification' of rural Britain since World War II?[3] If that kind of 'instant history' is too daunting, we can certainly amplify the evidence to be left behind (ensuring that journalists, politicians and bureaucrats will not be the only sources of information for future local historians). Thus, some county organisations encourage specially appointed recorders to make notes, build up

---

[1] N. Evans in *TLH*, 22, 4 (Nov. 1992), 203-07; M. Manson in *TLH*, 25, 2 (May, 1995), 66-76; M. Crick in *JORALS*, 12, 1 (1992), 1-17.
[2] Phythian-Adams has argued that students should be made to experience the sheer length of history, while Marshall stresses the value of teaching history backwards: Marshall, *Tyranny of the Discrete*, p.123.
[3] For example, Bill Goodhand's case study of Welbourn, which is Chapter 12 of D. R. Mills (ed.), *Twentieth Century Lincolnshire* (History of Lincolnshire, xii, 1989). Another good example, though from a different discipline, is the work of folklorists on the extraordinary national and local events which surrounded the death and funeral of Diana, Princess of Wales, in 1997: *Folklore*, 109 (1998).

scrap-books and take photographs.[1] This approach is of great personal benefit: *from the contemporary world of which we form part, we as historians derive not only our curiosity about the human condition, but also our awareness of how truth gets clouded and evidence is lost.*[2]

GROUP-WORK

Although most local history is written by individuals, and always will be, research and writing can also be done successfully by groups. After a subject has been agreed, basic tasks such as transcribing and analysing can be shared out, and the difficulties of interpretation discussed by all participants. Careful supervision and checking are obviously essential to ensure consistent standards and, if the ultimate aim is to publish, it is advisable that one person should co-ordinate the work and be in overall editorial control.[3] The great justification of group-work is that it helps to overcome the isolation of much historical research, and harnesses the energies and abilities of those who may not have produced much by themselves. For example, some local history societies, wishing to go beyond the normal routine of lectures and excursions, organise research projects and publish their results. In Kent the Faversham Society has produced over sixty titles including church guides, transcribed records and thematic studies. Group-work has also been a marked feature in adult education, from the 1960s to '80s especially, when classes embarked on 'participatory history' by turning themselves into research groups and working under the direction of a tutor.[4]

Sometimes groups of historians do productive work on a much larger scale, regionally or even nationally. Such projects are usually planned and steered by a few professionals, but they crucially depend on the industry and abilities of many part-timers. As is well known, hundreds of local historians from all over the country were drawn into the work of the Cambridge Group for the History of Population and Social Structure, and have contributed by transcribing parish registers and other sources, and by undertaking standardised types of analysis.[5] Over a period of six years 118 individuals in Herefordshire recorded and mapped over 125,000 field-names in 260 parishes, and in 1994 won a national archaeological award. A survey

---

[1] V. Norrington, *Recording the Present* (BALH, 1989).
[2] A related phenomenon is the 'Black Book', which for legal reasons is not published in the author's lifetime but is left in a safe place to await the verdict of posterity. I have known two people who have chosen this way of commenting on contemporary life.
[3] A. Rogers (ed.), *Group Projects in Local History* (Dawson, 1977). The same point applies to joint authorship: in practice each author, by prior arrangement, usually writes his own sections or chapters, but it is still advisable for one diplomatic person to be responsible for the overall shaping.
[4] A. Rogers, 'Participatory Research in Local History', *JORALS*, 15 (1995), 1-14.
[5] E. A. Wrigley & R. S. Schofield, *The Population History of England, 1541-1871* (1981), pp. 5-6. This book was dedicated 'To the local population historians of England'.

of migration in Britain from the 18th to 20th centuries, including movement over very short distances within towns, was recently achieved with the assistance of nearly 1400 family historians. In Hertfordshire scores of local and family historians are working with academics, archivists and librarians to help establish 'a computerised resource base' for the county's history, using documents such as parish registers, the census enumerations of 1851, and registers of union workhouses.[1]

Some people might regard such projects as unscrupulous exploitation: professionals using the goodwill of amateurs to get donkey-work done. That this is not necessarily the case has been proved conclusively by *Local Population Studies*, the journal of the Cambridge Group. Since its foundation in 1968 this unpretentious periodical has become a worthy monument to fruitful co-operation between professional and part-time historians. Indeed it has helped to blur that distinction by showing that 'amateurs' not only do basic tasks well but can genuinely contribute to knowledge and academic debate.[2]

AIDS TO RESEARCH AND TEACHING

Original reconstructions of the past are not the only forms of writing to be considered. The value of gathering contemporary evidence for the benefit of future generations has already been mentioned. Another important job is the compiling of indexes: in every part of Britain, the usefulness of many books, journals, newspapers, photographic collections and record publications is reduced by their having no indexes, or only poor ones. When a new index is compiled, preferably subdivided into People, Places and Subjects (see below, pp. 80-1), it can easily be duplicated, if not actually printed, and should certainly be deposited in local libraries and record offices.

A related problem is that we often lack bibliographical information. Only a few counties, such as Kent and Oxfordshire, have full-scale bibliographies listing all kinds of published material. This is admittedly an enormous task to undertake, and it still leaves the problem of updating as new publications thump from the press.[3] Easier to achieve are shorter, more selective and critical bibliographies on individual topics

---

[1] *LHM*, 52 (Nov-Dec 1995), 16-20; C. G. Pooley & J. Turnbull, *Migration and Mobility in Britain since the 18th Century* (1998); N. Goose, 'Participatory and Collaborative Research in English Regional and Local History: The Hertfordshire Historical Resources Project', *Archives*, xxii, 97 (Oct. 1997), 98-110. Another example of co-operation using hundreds of local volunteers is the National Inventory of War Memorials, managed by the Imperial War Museum and RCHM (England): C. Moriarty, *TLH*, 20, 3 (Aug. 1990), 123-5.

[2] The biographical notes given with articles in this journal are always worth reading: they often reveal that the authors, though technically 'amateurs', are experienced and well qualified in a host of different ways. On the debit side, it needs saying that this journal contains many examples of bad writing and weak editing.

[3] This is normally done by producing supplements. For example, E. H. Cordeaux & D. H. Merry, *A Bibliography of Printed Works relating to Oxfordshire* (Oxford Hist. Soc., ns xi, 1955); *Supplement* (ns xxviii, 1981); *A Bibliography of Printed Works relating to the City of Oxford* (Oxford Hist. Soc., ns xxv, 1976). Computerisation will of course make it easier to produce supplements.

such as agricultural change, the Reformation or the Lancashire cotton industry. These are of course regularly compiled by academics for their students in seminars and lecture-courses, but regrettably they are not given the wider currency they deserve by organisations like the Historical Association. We also need more abstracts summarising and evaluating books and articles as they appear (see below, p. 37-8).

Lastly we come to the vital job of preparing 'record' publications. This of course entails the transcribing or abstracting (and sometimes translation) of original documents for the benefit of students, teachers and scholars. At one end of the scale full-blown volumes are published by record societies serving individual counties, regions or the whole country. This admirable work continues though it is often supported by perilously small numbers of subscribers.[1] At the other end are articles or 'notes' in a journal or newsletter, a pack or archive unit, or simply a duplicated set of transcripts. Whatever the document and form of publication, the addition of critical notes always helps a reader to appreciate the character of the original, its provenance, the information offered, and problems of interpretation. For example, the recent Phillimore edition of Domesday Book, though it has irritating features, carries indexes and notes which undoubtedly improve the average person's access to, and use of, that difficult text.

Many local historians, instead of dissipating their energies on wide-ranging and unfocused research, would be better advised to publish key documents for their own localities.[2] This is also a task which can be done well by local societies (other than specifically 'record societies'). For example, since its foundation in 1957 the Banbury Historical Society in Oxfordshire has not only produced well over a hundred issues of its magazine *Cake and Cockhorse*, but up to 1995 had published twenty-five volumes of local records including parish registers, corporation books, wills, churchwardens' accounts and protestation returns.[3]

---

[1] One of the most public-spirited things any historically-minded person can do, is to subscribe to a record society. Most counties have such an organisation.

[2] For example, F. H. Erith, *Ardleigh in 1796* (1978), which publishes the detailed census of an Essex parish, and R. L. Sawyer, *The Bowerchalke Parish Papers: Collett's Village Newspaper, 1878-1924* (Alan Sutton, 1989) which samples a remarkable parish magazine from Wiltshire.

[3] In this connection we should remember that family historians are now producing an impressive array of record publications and introductions to sources.

4. THE SEARCH FOR SOURCES

The task is fraught with immense difficulty, for the historian is never allowed to invent; he must always find evidence for his statements.
(Joan Thirsk, in M. K. Ashby, *The Changing English Village*, 1974, xv)

For over forty years books, pamphlets and articles have been written on this aspect of research, and undoubtedly many more will follow. The search for new evidence, and for new uses of old evidence, never ends. Some older books of a general kind are still well worth consulting, such as W. G. Hoskins, *Local History in England* (3rd edn, 1984), W. B. Stephens, *Sources for English Local History* (2nd edn, 1981) and Alan Macfarlane, *A Guide to English Historical Records* (1983). Especially helpful is Philip Riden's *Record Sources for Local History* (2nd edn, 1998). This broad approach is kept alive by the Historical Association's re-issued *Short Guides to Records*, edited by Lionel Munby and Kate Thompson (1994 and 1998).

In parallel with these introductions, and fast becoming the norm, are more special-ised guides of two main kinds. The first group deals with particular sources, or groups of sources, such as P. D. A. Harvey, *Manorial Records* (1984), J. Gibson *et al.*, *Poor Law Union Records* (1993) and R. Hoyle, *Tudor Taxation Records* (1994).[1] The second group explores the sources for broad themes such as Peter Edwards, *Farming: Sources for Local Historians* (1991) and A. Morton, *Education and the State from 1833* (1997).[2] Nor should we forget that county record offices still publish guides to their own collect-ions,[3] that journals like *The Local Historian* and *The Journal of Regional and Local Studies* frequently publish articles about particular kinds of evidence, and that important leads can be found in *VCH* volumes, especially through their numerous footnotes.

---

[1] Well over a hundred such guides, often written by the indefatigable Jeremy Gibson, have been published in booklet form by the Federation of Family History Societies. Other well-known series are associated with the names of Eve McLaughlin and Colin Chapman. Though intended primarily for family historians, such guides can be of considerable value for local history. The PRO also has useful leaflets for many of its major classes of record.

[2] Guides to subjects, and to sources, are regularly published by the PRO (Reader's Guides), the British Records Association (Archives and the User), the Historical Manuscripts Commission (Guides to Sources for British History) and the Historical Geography Research Group (Research Series). A good bibliography of such guides, compiled by G. C. F. Forster, can be found in the *Short Guides to Records* (Historical Assocn, 1994 and 1998).

[3] For example, Derbyshire in 1994 and Cornwall in 1995.

Public access to original manuscripts has been revolutionised in the last half-century. Indeed, searchers of all kinds are now positively welcomed at record offices and local-studies libraries.[1] To some cynics, 'never have so many historically untrained people come into contact with so many documents'[2] but, viewed more charitably, the rapid development of record offices has had mostly good effects. Contact with real historical sources has been hugely valuable in personal and educational terms: it has given searchers direct experience of the past, taught them the rudiments of historical method, and stimulated practical research. Less desirably, it has deluded some people into thinking that history is simply the study of original documents: we merely have to look at manuscripts, get them xeroxed and the job is done. This is a dangerous fallacy, which gives rise to an uncritical worship of documents, common in certain educational circles. Not only are some documents dull, repetitive and comparatively unrevealing, but sources in general only become meaningful when the user has a clear sense of direction. In public searchrooms, it is noticeable that experienced historians skim through large numbers of documents for wide geographical areas, searching for evidence which is strictly relevant to their purposes; in doing so, they reject far more than they accept. By contrast, many beginners doggedly plough through (and transcribe) everything they can find relating to their own village or town, sturdily refusing to look at anything else. This may have its uses, but displays a fundamental reluctance to weigh evidence and solve specific problems.

It is not the purpose of this book to discuss the potentialities of particular manuscript or printed sources, but five general points about the search for evidence ought to be mentioned, because they inevitably affect the quality of our research and writing.

PRINTED PRIMARY SOURCES

Transcribed sources and edited texts must be approached with the same caution as raw manuscripts. We must remember that transcription and editing have not always been of the high standard we expect today. Editors have been known not only to make mistakes but also to select, omit, alter, add and translate freely — all without proper acknowledgement.[3] Even with a perfect transcription, an editor always stands between us and the original manuscript. We rely on him for our appreciation of the 'archaeology' of the document — the material of which it is made, its state of preservation, the character of the handwriting, the physical context in which it was found. Nevertheless, most major libraries contain several series of

---

[1] In 1980 few searchers would have guessed that, before the end of the century, the PRO might have a series of popularly written Reader's Guides, including one called 'Never Been Here Before?'
[2] Marshall, *Tyranny of the Discrete*, p. 47.
[3] The publications of the Record Commissioners contain some interesting flaws. In their transcription of the Hundred Rolls (*Rotuli Hundredorum*, ii, 499), published in 1818, the nunnery of CHATERIS (Cambs.) appears as OKACERIF: L. Munby, *Reading Tudor and Stuart Handwriting* (1988), p. 5.

printed transcripts which can yield valuable evidence for every local historian. Obvious examples include official calendars produced by the PRO, the work of the Record Commissioners and Historical Manuscripts Commission, and the regular editions of record societies, both national and local (Appendix 1, pp. 90-1).[1] *It is regrettable that although local historians can be very knowledgeable about manuscript sources, they often know comparatively little about those in print.* If they were more willing to comb the latter, particularly those which are well indexed, they would find not only new evidence for their own research, but also highly instructive parallels from other places and periods.

SECONDARY SOURCES: THE WORK OF OTHER HISTORIANS

This point, though it may seem merely an extension of the last, cannot be over-emphasised. *We must never forget the value of wide reading in and around our chosen subject and period (that is, the relevant 'historiography'). Indeed we should start with such reading, and continue it for as long as the work lasts.*[2] The reading of secondary printed literature has several beneficial effects. It helps to avoid unnecessary duplication, leads to the discovery of other comparative studies, and gives background knowledge which powerfully influences our own reconstruction of the past. This is how, for example, we judge when local events were reflections of national life, when they were part of regional trends, and when they were uniquely local.[3]

An awareness of historiography constantly reminds us that we are not working on our own, and that history is a cumulative, never-ending search for the truth. Because we do not necessarily agree with all that we read, we are also reminded that our work may contribute to wider historical debates. In fact, a well-researched project does not merely touch the work of other people, but grows out of it. By tending to work from secondary sources to primary, we deliberately move from cultivated ground to uncultivated, from the partially known to the entirely unknown. In this way we avoid the aimless accumulation of information for its own sake. On the contrary, we immediately see potential in our evidence, and begin to work with economy and direction. After persistent and well-chosen reading, it is inevitable that one's writing is transformed for the better. It is no accident that most articles and books begin by reviewing the work of other historians: by summarising their

---

[1] Printed sources such as newspapers and parliamentary papers are not included here, because they must be treated in the same way as manuscripts: no modern editor or transcriber has intervened.
[2] A. Rogers, 'Reading about Local History', *LHM*, 36 (Nov-Dec 1992), 19.
[3] An obvious example lies in the effect of parliamentary legislation. When a parish is found to have built a workhouse in the early 18th century, it should be seen in the light of the Workhouse Test Act of 1723 which positively encouraged such initiatives. Similarly, when we read in 16th-century church-wardens' accounts of the removal of images, stone altars, relics, plate and vestments, we have to be aware of the acts, ordinances and injunctions which drove the English Reformation.

discoveries and opinions, one makes room for a new contribution. Thereafter, good writers frequently return to what others have written, as a means of developing their own ideas and fitting them into a web of existing research.[1]

We should approach secondary historical literature as we would grandfather's diary or tomorrow's *Guardian*. They are someone's version of the past, and not in any sense holy writ. Because historians have a duty to interpret, and to use their evidence with controlled imagination, they often disagree. At first this may seem an embarrassment, but disagreements and historical controversies frequently lead to significant advances in knowledge — because scholars stimulate each other to think again, to ask new questions, to analyse sources more deeply, or to seek entirely new evidence. We have to overcome the instinctive assumption that if something is in print it is 'right'.

The amount of history now being published in books and journals is truly daunting, not to speak of pamphlets, bulletins and newsletters. For the local historian, the problem is compounded by the width of his interests, for he rightly tries to keep in touch with a wide range of specialisations. In practice, the best chance of coping lies in scanning references, bibliographies and reviews. Most national journals contain reviews and lists of recent publications, though one should always remember that a review may not appear for several years.[2] Especially valuable are historiographical articles which 'round up' the latest and most significant work on a particular subject.[3] Among the more obvious periodicals to comb regularly for reviews are *The Local Historian* (published by the British Association for Local History), *History* (published by the Historical Association), *Archives* (published by the British Records Association), and regional or national journals such as *Northern*, *Midland* and *Southern History*, *The Scottish Historical Review* and *The Welsh History Review*. According to one's interests it also pays to consult periodicals which are more thematically specialised, for example *Local Population Studies*, *The Economic History Review*, *Social History*, *Urban History* and *The Journal of Ecclesiastical History*.[4]

Where they exist, abstracts (brief summaries) of books and articles can be a valuable guide and time-saver. They appear in three principal forms: with individual articles

---

[1] The principal reason why essays and dissertations receive lower marks than their writers expect, is an insuffiency of background and general reading.

[2] *The Local History Magazine* edited from Nottingham by Susan and Robert Howard, and produced six times a year, is often first off the mark with reviews and notices of new publications.

[3] For example, Clive Field's review of work on the religious census of 1851 (*TLH*, 27, 4, Nov. 1997, 194-217). The *Annual Bulletin of Historical Literature: A Critical Review of New Publications*, published by the Historical Association, divides British history by period and subject.

[4] For example, the *Economic History Review* and *Agricultural History Review* publish lists of recent books and articles which contain subdivisions such as Local History, County and Regional History and Original Documents.

in journals, as annual or occasional round-ups, and in a few special periodicals.[1] Although more journals are now appending these summaries to their articles, a good case can be made for the establishment of a national series of abstracts concentrating on local and regional history.

Appendix 1 on pp. 90-3 gives more information on printed sources, both primary and secondary. Here it is enough to say that they include books and journals of general and national history; histories of parishes, towns, counties and regions; biographies, diaries and journals; official calendars or summaries of original documents; lists and indexes of national archives; the publications of record societies; county historical and archaeological journals; volumes of notes and queries; newspapers and ephemera; maps, engravings and photographs. In this quest, the assistance of experienced librarians (including 'local studies' specialists) is of great importance.[2] *The creative local historian should spend at least as much time on books and journals as on manuscripts and other forms of original evidence.*[3]

MAKING HUMAN CONTACTS

Anyone committed to research and writing must seek contact with people who may be able to help, whether in the finding of evidence, in its interpretation, in suggesting relevant reading, or in commenting helpfully on drafts. Of course students writing dissertations automatically receive supervision, but outside formal courses contacts may include archivists, librarians, archaeologists, place-name specialists, genealogists, geographers, botanists and art historians, to mention but a few. Furthermore, we must gain the confidence of any person who may show us private collections, give us access to places normally inaccessible, or recall useful memories. But the most valuable links are undoubtedly with other historians. For example, much information and many sources are found by accident, and *if we hope that others will note references which may be useful to us, we must be prepared to do the same for them.*

---

[1] See, for example, recent issues of the *Agricultural History Review, Economic History Review* and *Urban History*. In some journals the abstract appears at the head of each article, and in others at the beginning of each issue. *The Welsh History Review* has an excellent series of short abstracts collected on an annual basis. The *British and Irish Archaeological Bibliography*, published twice a year, contains abstracts relating to local history. Useful information can also be got from wider-ranging abstracts. *The British Humanities Index* is a quarterly guide to articles in British journals and newspapers; it surveys most national and regional (not county) journals of history and archaeology. *Historical Abstracts* is a quarterly which surveys 'the world's historical literature' in two main series, A (1450-1914) and B (1914 to the present), each with a good index.

[2] See Diana Winterbotham & A. Crosby, *The Local Studies Library: A Handbook for Local Historians* (BALH, 1998).

[3] A welcome modern trend is to bring record offices and local-studies libraries together in the same building.

Such help clearly depends on good personal relations, and on the regular exchange of news and views. If they do not already exist, opportunities should be created for local historians to meet and talk, not only in purely local societies but, more importantly, at a county or regional level. Good examples are the regular lectures and seminars organised by various universities, some in centres of regional history, which enable professionals and part-timers to discuss current or completed research. Major conferences and history fairs can also be useful in this way. The essential point is that *an individual who is isolated is inevitably restricting his own development as an historian, and anyone intending to write cannot afford to be without such help and support.* Naturally, whenever significant help of any kind is received, it should be acknowledged as a matter of honesty and courtesy.

PHYSICAL EVIDENCE

By definition, an historian's basic task is to interpret verbal evidence. This he will find in manuscripts produced in the course of everyday life, in sources which have been edited and published, in oral evidence which is now firmly within the historian's domain, and in the rapidly growing mountain of secondary literature by which generations of historians have attempted to reconstruct the past. The sensitive local historian, however, will also be conscious of the landscape which surrounds him, a vast complex of physical features created by successive generations as they adapted their environment according to their economic resources and technical abilities.

For example, how can anyone writing about religious beliefs neglect the fabric and furnishings of local churches and chapels?[1] In a discussion of living conditions in the past, how can anyone overlook vernacular buildings, or the excavation of buried settlements? Similarly, is it possible for a student of farming to omit all reference to soils, relief and drainage, the changing shapes and sizes of fields, earthworks like lynchets and ridge-and-furrow, and the patterns revealed by aerial photography? All these features are not merely of antiquarian interest, but are serious historical evidence of human thought and decisions. Yet it is amazing how often, for instance, economic historians writing about markets or fairs have ignored their physical characteristics and setting. In doing so, they have wilfully omitted evidence germane to their subjects. (Incidentally, certain kinds of 'visual' document such as maps, engravings and old photographs may prove vital in linking the material world to ordinary written sources.)

Nobody expects the local historian to become an expert in fundamentally different disciplines, for example, in architectural history or field archaeology. Furthermore,

---

[1] The argument cuts both ways. How is it possible for someone studying ecclesiastical architecture to neglect liturgical practices and religious belief?

without adequate training it is dangerous to blunder into a highly specialised field like the study of place-names. Nevertheless, with his catholic approach to the past the local historian should consider other forms of evidence and draw on the knowledge and publications of other specialists — where they are relevant to his own interests and where two or more kinds of evidence can be usefully combined. *While recognising the perils of stepping into less familiar territory, we must be flexible enough to follow where our subject leads.* Above all, this means having the confidence to approach other kinds of specialist.

THE STORAGE OF INFORMATION

The local historian must teach himself the elementary techniques of finding and storing information. For example, without reading every word he must 'gut' printed books to assess their value, by skimming contents-pages, forewords, conclusions and indexes. He must become familiar with the conventions behind transcripts, translations, calendars and bibliographies; and must know how to use indexes and catalogues in libraries and record offices, whether they be in the form of books, files, card-indexes, microfilm or CD-ROM. These are skills which we should all have been taught at school but, alas, seldom were until quite recently. Fortunately, librarians and archivists are usually prepared to explain how their reference-systems work — if asked at a convenient moment — or they can provide introductory leaflets. It is significant that most postgraduates beginning research today need an introduction to 'study skills' of this kind.

Historians obviously need an efficient system of note-taking. Many able people never write because their information is badly recorded and stored. It is asking for trouble to scribble on odd bits of paper and the 'backs of envelopes'. If, on the other hand, one fills up notebooks with hundreds of miscellaneous facts and references, one simply buries the information yet again, and complicates the business of retrieval at a later stage. Admittedly time should not be spent on unnecessary organisation, but very few historians court that danger! In practice most of us improvise rather reluctantly as the raw materials, in whatever form, threaten to engulf us.

In the last two decades, historical research has been revolutionised by the adoption of the word-processor, with its ever-improving speed and memory. Not only is this piece of modern technology increasingly used in writing and editing, but it is proving invaluable for the storage, retrieval and analysis of historical information, principally in the form of databases and spreadsheets. In record offices and libraries — providing enough electrical sockets are available — the portable 'laptop' is now a common sight (and sound). With this machine, the researcher can cut out intermediate tasks and dispense with traditional pencils, rubbers and paper. He can, for example, put transcripts of original documents straight into the machine's memory and print-out any number of copies; or he can immediately transfer data from manuscripts to a previously prepared form of analysis. For example, details from tithe apportionments can be directly allotted to an unlimited number of headed columns in a spreadsheet, containing either numbers or words, or both.[1]

For reasons of finance, age or temperament, however, some historians will always prefer to work in traditional ways. A good 'manual' method, developed long ago by the staff of the *VCH*, can still be adapted to most circumstances. Basically, each discovered 'fact' with its reference and a short heading is put on a separate slip of paper. Slips, all of the same size, are stored in a filing cabinet (or a cheap substitute like shoe-boxes). As the collection grows, it can be divided into obvious categories with appropriate sub-headings: Church, Market, Public Health, Disorder, etc. When it comes to writing on a particular topic, the relevant slips can be pulled out, perhaps from several subdivisions, re-read and arranged in logical order.[2] An advantage of slips is that they can be run through quickly, like bank-notes. On the other hand, cards are more hard-wearing and stand better in a box. As a further refinement some researchers use slips or cards of different colours: each colour is devoted to a major aspect of the subject, and this may help with sorting. Nevertheless, other historians choose quite different methods: loose-leaf files, box-files, envelope-files, heaps on the floor, and so on. Needless to say, all quotations and transcripts must be made accurately, so that one does not in any way misrepresent what a source says. Finally, because the progress of research is not predictable, one has to be ready to incorporate new and unexpected developments. This means that, *whatever system of recording is adopted, manual or technological, it must be flexible, easy to sort and capable of both expansion and subdivision.*

Whether one is computerised or not, it is always a good idea to make a separate record of sources. Every time a major document, article or book is found, all its details should be noted, with its reference in the appropriate record office or library. Thereafter, any information derived from that source need only bear an abbreviated reference. Thus, one's index of sources might contain: David Rollison, *The Local Origins of Modern Society: Gloucestershire, 1500-1800* (Routledge, 1992). Individual references taken from the same book need only carry: Rollison, *Local Origins*, 46, or Rollison (1992), 46.

---

[1] Software manuals are notoriously difficult to follow. Nevertheless, helpful introductions to the mysteries of word-processing can be found in some recently published books. See Bibliography on p. 88.

[2] R. B. Pugh, *How to Write a Parish History* (1954), pp. 136-9. Of course, the logical order of slips will not necessarily be chronological (see above, p. 64).

5. TRANSCRIBING

Faced with an original document, the historian's first task is to transcribe the written message, or that part of it, which he wants to use. In many cases this means no more than careful reading and accurate copying. The earlier the document, however, and the less familiar the handwriting, the more necessary are the skills of the palaeographer. In practice, for many researchers, this means grappling with the Secretary Hand of the Tudor and Stuart period. Yet even with quite modern documents, a measure of palaeography is always needed: for example the long 's' was still being used in the 19th century, and most local historians have been baffled by certain words written in the tight copperplate of census enumerators in 1841 and 1851. Moreover, in every generation individuals had their own idiosyncracies of style, and some wrote hurriedly and badly. This is a reminder that *palaeography always involves two styles: that of the period and that of the writer*.

This book is no place for a detailed discussion of handwriting and its elucidation. Fortunately several good manuals are available, covering both the medieval and early modern periods. Not only do they explain the normal forms of lower-case and capital letters, but also deal with related problems like ligatures (joined letters), the survival of Anglo-Saxon characters (especially the thorn and yogh; see p. 96), Roman and Arabic numerals, and the troublesome habit of abbreviation. Even the simplest manuals, which usually provide facsimiles on one page with a full transcript opposite, are sufficient to motivate the novice who is willing to practise.[1]

In the last resort, palaeography is not so much taught as learnt. Every stroke of the pen and mark on the paper have to be understood, even if they turn out to be unimportant — like a space-filler, the 'pip' on the end of a bracket, an ink-blot or an imperfection in the paper itself. The modern xerox machine is a blessing for it enables us to practise at home on documents which we positively want to crack. We can begin

---

[1] For example, F. G. Emmison, *How to Read Local Archives, 1550-1700* (Historical Association, 1967); H. Grieve, *Examples of English Handwriting, 1150-1750* (Essex Record Office, 1954); L. Munby, *Reading Tudor and Stuart Handwriting* (British Association for Local History, 1988); R. C. Newton, *Medieval Local Records* (Historical Association, 1971). More detailed are G. E. Dawson & L. Kennedy-Skipton, *Elizabethan Handwriting, 1500-1650* (1968); L. C. Hector, *The Handwriting of English Documents* (1958); E. Danbury, *Palaeography for Historians* (Phillimore, 1999). For abbreviations, see C. Trice Martin, *The Record Interpreter* (Phillimore reprint, 1994).

with relatively easy examples and then, motivated by success, tackle more demanding ones. In adult classes students can usually, after a few weeks' persistence and hard work, acquire the expertise to read documents back to the early sixteenth century. A few go much further and in time become competent readers of medieval palaeography.

It is vital to develop good habits from the start. (Let us take for granted good light, the right spectacles, a magnifying glass, a copy of an 'alphabet' showing the different forms of each letter,[1] and perhaps access to an ultra-violet lamp.) A fundamental principle is that we must not guess or muddle through, but read slowly, deliberately and comparatively. If a letter is difficult to interpret, look for the same character elsewhere in the same document where it may be clearer. In reading historical documents one frequently asks oneself questions such as: how does this scribe normally write his lower-case 'r' or capital 'S'?

Transcriptions of documents are usually made in one of three ways. Although a fast-growing minority type directly into 'laptops', the majority of searchers in record offices still (in 1999!) make a copy in longhand using the required pencil.[2] A few, at the risk of disturbing other searchers, dictate their reading into tape-recorders and later transcribe their tapes.[3] If (like me) you are still a manuscript transcriber, remember to write in a large, clear and well-spaced hand. Otherwise at a later stage, details may be easily misconstrued. For example a hastily scrawled transcript may fail to distinguish 'c' from 't', '3' from '5', or capitals from lower-case letters.

If you are stuck over a particular word, leave a space in your transcription and read on. Sometimes a later line will give the same word in a clearer form, or the general context will suggest a meaning. Even if neither happens, the mere act of leaving and later returning with a fresh eye often leads to success: what had been a shapeless squiggle is now suddenly understandable. But even the most skilled palaeographer will sometimes be defeated, and must honestly admit failure by leaving a gap or writing *illegible* (or *illeg.*). Sometimes we may provide a reading but are not entirely sure of it. Here a question-mark should be inserted immediately *before* the word or number, once again in the interests of honesty and accuracy. [All such editorial insertions should be placed within square brackets.] One final point of great importance. Having transcribed a document, re-check your transcript against the original at least once, because errors can easily creep in. And check it again if

---

[1] As in H. Grieve (1954), Fig.1, and L. Munby (1988), pp. 4, 7-10.
[2] By far the easiest method is to use a good-quality propelling pencil, which eliminates the tedious use of pencil-sharpeners. Another vital piece of equipment for the transcriber of manuscripts is of course a rubber, preferably of the new pencil shape because it can be used quite delicately.
[3] Technologically it is possible that scanners, in the not-too-distant future, will be able to produce transcripts of manuscripts, as they can already do for printed materials. Will they ever be able to produce reliable translations?

you go on to publish it, or quote from it. See Appendix 3 on pp. 96-7 for the basic rules and conventions for transcribing original documents.[1]

Where documents were written in a language other than English, the historian will also have to translate. He will certainly do this mentally as he reads and transcribes his source, but at a later stage he may also need to write a formal translation — especially if it enables him to bring a significant document to the attention of a wider audience. While the palaeographer is concerned with symbols or characters, the translator focuses on the meaning of words. At this point, the complexities of historical interpretation begin to appear: our understanding of what the writer meant to convey starts with his choice of words. In practice the foreign language which the local historian is most likely to meet is Latin, which continued to be used in legal documents until 1733. Fortunately we have good aids in R. E. Latham's *Medieval Latin Word-List* (last revised in 1965) and the *Dictionary of Medieval Latin from British Sources*.[2] It is also advisable to have access to classical dictionaries such as C. T. Lewis and C. Short, *A Latin Dictionary* (last impression 1991) and the *Oxford Latin Dictionary* (2 vols, 1968 and 1976). For those with no knowledge of Latin, or who need to revise the Latin of their schooldays, the best manuals are Eileen Gooder's *Latin for Local Historians* (1961), David Gosden's *Starting to Read Medieval Latin Manuscript* (1993), Denis Stuart's *Latin for Local and Family Historians* (1995) and that old faithful, B. H. Kennedy's *The Revised Latin Primer* (last reprinted in 1986).

An element of translation is necessary in the reading of any document, even relatively modern ones written in English. This is because words are constantly changing in meaning and emphasis. Just think of the traps waiting for the unwary in the following:
- 'prevent' which formerly meant 'go before'
- 'honest' meaning 'competent'
- 'steeple' meaning 'tower'
- 'carpet' meaning 'table cloth' or 'covering'
- 'indifferent' meaning 'impartial'
- 'incontinently' which in the Middle Ages meant 'without delay'; later meant 'unlawfully' or 'sinfully'; and finally became associated with bodily malfunctions.[3]

---

[1] Every teacher of palaeography remembers spectacular howlers. Instead of the familiar phrase in early wills, 'for tithes forgotten', I was once offered 'for tips for Satan'. A relatively common error is to transcribe the English word 'eme' meaning 'uncle' as a woman's name: 'myn *Emma* and myn awnte'.
[2] The *Dictionary of Medieval Latin from British Sources*, published by the British Academy, has (in 1999) got to the letter 'L'.
[3] A dramatic recent example is the fate of that little word 'gay' which, in a decade or less, acquired a completely new meaning and lost its traditional one.

In addition, documents often contain dialect words and technical language, all of which have to be understood. Here again, help can be found in key reference books. If the full *Oxford English Dictionary* does not provide the answer, as it usually does, then turn to Joseph Wright's *English Dialect Dictionary* (6 vols, 1898-1905), J. O. Halliwell's *Dictionary of Archaisms and Regionalisms* (2 vols, 1847), *A Medieval Farming Glossary of Latin and English Words* (revised by A. & R. Powell, Essex Record Office, 1998) and the indispensable *Middle English Dictionary* which is nearing completion. Similar help can be found in Joy Bristow's *Local Historian's Glossary* (1994), and in David Hey's *Oxford Companion to Local and Family History* (1996) which is in effect a dictionary.

Those historians who compile glossaries of local and regional words undoubtedly perform a valuable service for others. Fortunately this habit seems to be spreading, in record publications and elsewhere.[1] When words are rare or important historically, glossaries should be cross-referenced in two ways: to the published dictionaries which help to explain them, and to the folios or pages where they occur in an original document or record publication (see Appendix 22, pp. 158-9). It should be noted that the *Oxford English Dictionary* (3rd edition) now incorporates information from local record publications. These often reveal forms of words earlier than those in literary texts, and even totally new words. Here, once again, local history is contributing to a different specialisation.[2]

Frequently, however, working historians do not transcribe or translate *every* word in the manuscripts they study. They often choose to create a 'full abstract', which is a careful summary in modern English.[3] In this way they record all significant statements in a more compact form. For example, wills contain a great deal of repetitive verbiage such as 'Item I leave and bequeath ...' and 'The residue of all my goods and chattels', so they are commonly abstracted (Appendix 4, pp. 103-4). The danger is that one might omit details which later turn out to be important, for example the opening religious clauses of 16th-century wills which have recently been the subject of vigorous controversy. This means that abstracts should only be made when one is thoroughly familiar with a particular class of record. Within a full abstract most historians choose to transcribe certain words and phrases *exactly*,

---

[1] For example, N. W. Alcock, *People at Home: Living in a Warwickshire Village, 1500-1800* (1993), pp. 221-8; R. Milward, *A Glossary of Household, Farming and Trade Terms from Probate Inventories* (Derbyshire Record Soc., Occasional Paper No. 1, 1982); A. J. L. Winchester (ed.), *The Diary of Isaac Fletcher of Underwood, Cumberland, 1756-81* (Cumberland & Westmorland Antiq. & Archaeol. Soc., Extra Series xxv (1994), 453-7. A short but valuable glossary of north-eastern mining terms is included in D. Levine & K. Wrightson, *The Making of an Industrial Society: Whickham 1560-1765* (1991), 447-9.

[2] This particular 'reading project' is overseen by Dr Edmund Weiner of the *OED*. I am indebted to Kate Tiller for this point.

[3] In this book the term 'abstract' is used in two related senses, as meaning a) a summary or calendar of the contents of original documents, some more 'full' than others, and b) as a brief summary of published articles and books (see above, p. 37-8).

because they are worthy of quotation; these they distinguish by using inverted commas, italics or brackets.

Even more commonly, we find it sufficient to 'extract' those parts of documents which are relevant to our subject. For example, some historians comb churchwardens' accounts for references to poor relief, while others hunt for drama and festivities. The technique is the same as for making notes from printed sources. Again, it is usually important to transcribe particular words and phrases exactly, and one should always be careful to note the source of each extract (including page or folio, and date). *It is very easy to extract carelessly, failing to distinguish genuine quotations and omitting vital references. This either wastes time because one has to go back a second time to check details or, worse still, introduces error into one's writing.*

By all such methods (transcribing, translating, abstracting and extracting), one accumulates great quantities of handwritten notes or print-outs which have to be kept under control. Certainly paper should be of standard size, and properly filed so that items can be easily recovered when needed. One may choose to transfer salient details with appropriate references into a computerised database or spreadsheet, or into a separate card- or slip-index.[1] Alternatively the transcriptions themselves can be given various underlinings, asterisks, marginal headings and notes, so that useful information can be more easily retrieved when one comes to writing. Such additions should be distinguished from the original transcript by, for example, using a different writing material or colour. The same treatment can be given to xeroxes and other types of facsimile.

A NOTE ON DATING

When transcribing a document, the historian must be careful to note any kind of dating. The best policy, to avoid confusion at a later stage, is to transcribe the date *as given*, and then, if necessary, to give its modern equivalent in square brackets. Such conversions depend on knowing when the year began in the past (from the late-12th century until 1752, for example, the New Year in England began on Lady Day, 25 March); also the regnal years of kings and queens, the official years of popes, bishops and abbots, and above all the liturgical feasts of the Christian church. As a guide through this maze, we have C. R. Cheney's classic *Handbook of Dates* which first appeared in 1945 and is still kept in print (for its detailed use, see Appendix 5, pp. 105-6).[2]

---

[1] Every time one copies information or references, one increases the chance of making errors. All the more reason, therefore, to cross-check.

[2] For the official years of bishops, archbishops and holders of major offices of State, see E. B. Fryde *et al.* (eds), *Handbook of British Chronology* (CUP, 1996). Relevant volumes of the *VCH* give the official years of local abbots, priors, etc. under 'Religious Houses'. For popes, see Cheney (1995), pp. 33-9. For a general discussion of dating and useful lists and tables, see L. M. Munby, *Dates and Time: A Handbook for Local Historians* (BALH, 1997).

6. ANALYSING AND ASSEMBLING EVIDENCE

No document and no statement, official or non-official, is beyond question.
(G. Kitson Clark, *The Critical Historian*, 1967, p. 80)

Documents do not present the historian with established 'facts' or straightforward, reproducible 'truth'. Indeed we are doomed to failure if we merely collect pieces of information, and attempt to write history by stitching them together. *An historical document can only convey someone's version of what happened in the past, and it will assuredly mislead anyone who approaches it uncritically and with no sense of historical context.* The historian has a duty to interpret and find meaning in the past. Therefore he must read and re-read, always pondering on the significance of the words passing before his eyes. The main method of analysis is, first, for the historian to ask relevant and probing questions; and secondly, because the original writers cannot normally be re-interviewed, to work out as many answers as possible, for himself. Questions will be concerned with both the detail and general character of sources. 'In the use of archives, he finds the most who has some idea of what he is looking for.'[1]

The practical researcher, whatever his or her period of study, cannot remain entirely unaware of the historical science of Diplomatic. This critical technique was developed in the 19th century for investigating the origins and character of documents — particularly, as the word implies, the official diplomas and charters of the medieval period. The essential point is that the questions which a diplomatic historian might ask about a medieval charter should pass through the mind of any historian faced with original evidence. Who wrote it, or at least what kind of person wrote it? When, if only approximately, was it written? Why was it written? Does its physical character, say the handwriting, fit the alleged date? Are some of the statements second-hand and derived from earlier sources? Is it a copy? Or a copy of a copy? Is it a forgery?[2]

---

[1] G. C. F. Forster of Leeds University, in an unpublished paper read in October 1980 at a meeting convened by CORAL, to discuss methods and problems in the teaching of local history in higher education.

[2] In practice one of the most valuable applications of diplomatic technique is in identifying the work of early writers and antiquaries. The manuscripts of such people are often unsigned and undated; moreover at a later date they were frequently dispersed, re-arranged and copied. Dramatic examples are Diarmaid McCulloch's work on the so-called 'Chorography of Suffolk' written in about 1600, and Hassell Smith's re-assembling of the papers of Nathaniel Bacon of Stiffkey, Norfolk (1556-95). See D. N. J. MacCulloch, *The Chorography of Suffolk* (Suffolk Records Society, xix, 1976) and A. Hassell Smith, *The Papers of Nathaniel Bacon of Stiffkey* (3 vols, 1979, 1983 & 1990).

The whole process is a logical enquiry into the internal and external consistency of documents. It is not necessarily a process of rejecting some sources and accepting others. For example, forgeries may contain genuine and useful information; by contrast genuine documents do not necessarily tell the whole truth and are often most revealing of the writer's assumptions, priorities and prejudices, and of the system within which he was working. *The vast majority of historical documents were written for immediate and contemporary purposes, generally of an administrative or legal kind, and certainly not to supply evidence for future historians.*

So far as the character of a document is concerned, a whole succession of questions, general and particular, will arise in the mind of the critical historian as he attempts to assess the writer's purpose. For example:

- What parts of the document reflect the personality of the writer (his temperament, knowledge, ignorance, interests, emotions and prejudices)?
- What parts, if any, are determined by administrative procedures or by the conventions of the period?
- How far is the document based on first-hand experience; or derived at second or third hand? What parts appear to be guesswork and opinion?
- Does the document contain information which can be corroborated in other sources? Does it contain any unique information?
- What does the document *not* say? Does silence mean that something did not happen, or that it was consciously omitted?
- In general, how far can the contents be assessed in terms of truth, ambiguity, omission, distortion and falsehood? In a single document, any or all of these qualities can appear.

Central to all this probing is an attempt to enter the mind of the original writer. What did he mean and how did he know? Of more general interest, what were his motives and preoccupations when writing? Such enquiries do not constitute a secret method known only to professionals. They are the kinds of question which will occur to any thoughtful reader, or which any good teacher will try to stimulate in the minds of students faced with a literary text, a piece of music or a work of art. The whole purpose of this critical exercise is to assess the document's strengths, weaknesses and real historical significance (as opposed to its stated meaning). It should be noted that the questions themselves will not normally feature in one's writing. The answers, however, will inevitably colour the way one uses a particular source.

As has already been said, most documents come from an administrative system which had its own special procedures. These may not be immediately obvious when the historian first deals with a new class of record, but with experience he learns what kinds of information to expect and the language normally employed. Among other things, he comes to appreciate 'common form', the recurrent words and phrases which say more about the administrative system than about the individual case. When, for example, a pre-Reformation will mentions money bequeathed to the high altar of a parish church 'for tithes and offerings forgotten', it is not commenting on the shameful life of that particular testator, but is using a normal formula whereby the laity of this period compensated the clergy for inevitable lapses and forgetfulness. So in practice the answers to many critical questions will depend on the width of our experience and the depth of our background knowledge. Alternatively, for the beginner, it will depend on getting the right kind of advice, either from a more experienced historian or from suitable reading.

METHODS OF ANALYSIS

To wrestle with details *within* documents, we must again adopt the questioning approach. In the case of probate inventories we may ask: How many rooms did local houses contain? How were rooms named? How many rooms were heated? Is it possible to reconstruct the plans of ground-floors and first floors? Basic questions can lead to others of a more penetrating kind. For example, do furnishings reveal how rooms were used (e.g. for cooking, eating, sleeping, receiving guests, storage, etc.)? What were the dominant colours and textures in rooms? And so on. Our questions are not necessarily purely 'factual'. They often contain assumptions and judgements based on previous reading. For example, we presume that the presence of fire-irons in a room implies a fireplace; we are not told as much and could be wrong.

When dealing with a mass of documents, the historian is inevitably producing large quantities of paper in the form of notes, transcripts, xeroxed copies or print-outs. He is therefore forced by the sheer mass of information not only to store it efficiently but also to process it in a systematic way. Many different methods are possible, ranging from elementary to computerised, but they are all intended to sift, sort and re-assemble so that helpful distinctions can be made, and comparisons and generalisations built up. When all the information on a particular point has been gathered, the historian is in a much better position to make his own judgements and calculations, and thus turn the corner from mere analysis to creative interpretation.

How, therefore, do we handle all the verbal and numerical information in our documents? A common method is to draw up forms where details can be noted or counted in appropriate boxes or columns. Well-known examples for the analysis of parish registers are the printed forms designed by the Cambridge Group for the History of Population and Social Structure. They provide standardised ways of discovering overall trends in baptisms, marriages and burials, of identifying crises such as plague and dearth, of reconstituting families over generations, and of uncovering factors such as age at first marriage, fertility, family size, illegitimacy, and life expectancy. To return to inventories, different forms of analysis have been compiled for household furniture such as beds, tables and chairs, for stock-in trade such as the contents of shops and tools used by craftsmen, for various kinds of crops and animals belonging to farmers, and for luxuries such as glassware, silverware and clocks.

Of all forms of analysis, the most valuable are those which conflate information from two or more documents. Some historians, for instance, regularly devise forms or databases which bring together, for named individuals, evidence from wills, inventories, parish registers, hearth-tax returns, rate-books, poor-law examinations, and so on (Appendix 8, pp. 114-15). It should also be remembered that well designed analyses lead directly to the creation of figures, tables and graphs which are an important part of modern writing.

Historical analysis is now being revolutionised by the use of fast and powerful computers, allied to highly sophisticated software. The spread of scanners, moreover, ensures that documents can now be put straight into computers in their original printed or manuscript forms. Of course, before manuscripts can be analysed they still need to be transcribed and/or translated, but scanners in the future will probably do that too! As a result of this revolution, the present generation of historians can handle much larger quantities of data, and question and process them much faster. At Sowerby and Calverley in Yorkshire, for example, detailed computerised work on a wide variety of familiar sources is helping to reconstruct the lives of poor landless cottagers:

> we can now see how often and at what points in the life cycle they received poor relief; discover from whom they rented accommodation or land; identify the ways in which their occupations changed over time; and study the constant short distance movement which appears to have been characteristic of weavers and labourers in the townships. We can see who they married, how many children they had, how many died in childhood or became pauper apprentices …[1]

Across the whole of Britain an impressive variety of documents is now being computerised including parish registers, port books, hearth-tax and land-tax returns, wills and inventories, probate accounts, census enumerators' books, admission books for workhouses and prisons, urban rate books and trade directories — all of which are familiar to local historians. A project called Bristol Historical Databases has amassed many original sources for the city, including poll books, local obituaries and historical statistics, and makes them cheaply available on disk.[2] At Hull University, the whole of Domesday Book, which amounts to a million words, has been coded into a computer so that its various details (for example, the numbers of villeins and

---

[1] P. Hudson, 'A New History from Below: Computers and the Maturing of Local and Regional History', *TLH*, 25, 4 (Nov. 1995), 219.
[2] *Bristol Historical Databases Project Newsletter*, 6 (Dec. 1997), 3-5, 20-3.

sheep) can be assembled and counted. At the other end of the time-scale, work on conditions of labour, hours, wages and prices in different parts of the country, enables historians to expose, as never before, the uneven spread and complexity of the Industrial Revolution.

This technological revolution works for the local historian at several different levels. For example the computerised cataloguing and cross-referencing of archives are opening up new areas for exploration. Already it is possible for an individual from his own home to consult the catalogues of libraries and record offices. Once complete sources or extracts have been fed into a word processor ('inputted' is the ghastly jargon), details can be retrieved, re-ordered, linked to produce new knowledge, and even mapped. Of course the largest projects involve groups of academics and special funding, but some part-time historians are just as committed to this powerful new technology and just as proficient in its use.

No two people will draw up identical forms of analysis, whether manual or computerised, and there is no reason why they should. Documents are infinitely variable, and historians themselves have different priorities. A method has to be found which is appropriate to each task. In scale it must be large enough to wring useful generalisations from all relevant detail, but not so elaborate as to have almost as many headings as the document has details. The easiest documents to process are those which have standardised layouts like poll-books and census enumerations; the most difficult are those which have variable and unpredictable contents such as letters and personal journals. (Computerised and traditional kinds of analysis are illustrated in Appendices 6-9, pp. 107-17.)

Systematic analysis conveys another important advantage: it encourages us to make mathematical calculations. Certain classes of document contain many numbers, such as sums of money in accounts, while others present verbal information in such a repetitive way that it too can be quantified, as with types of offence brought before Quarter Sessions. The word 'cliometrics' is sometimes used to describe the mathematical revolution within history, and manuals are regularly written to encourage greater numeracy among historians.[1] Of course numbers and statistics must not be allowed to obscure the essential humanity of the subject, but at the same time we must not neglect any opportunity of giving our work greater precision.

But the most important benefit to flow from documentary analysis is to discover entirely new historical 'facts'. For example, in a classic article published in 1966 E. A. Wrigley showed that an outbreak of plague between November 1645 and October 1646 had killed 392 people in the the east Devon town of Colyton. He did not read that figure in any document; he worked it out by analysing hundreds of entries in a

---

[1] D. I. Greenstein, *A Historian's Guide to Computing* (1994); E. Mawdsley & T. Munck, *Computing for Historians; An Introductory Guide* (1993).

parish register. Then, by making certain assumptions about the birth-rate at that time, he calculated that those deaths represented about one-fifth of the whole population.[1] So by re-arranging and re-assembling information, the historian is able to create broader, more generalised or integrative facts. These usually prove valuable in writing because they 'boil down' detail which could never be presented in its original cumbersome form.

RELATING VARIED SOURCES

Historical research normally involves the use of several different kinds of evidence. Indeed this is welcomed by most people as a way of giving width and depth to a project. Therefore the historian regularly faces the problem of blending information from an assortment of documents, which were written from different points of view and for different purposes. Take for example the census returns, tithe apportionments and commercial directories which are widely used by students of 19th-century communities. Censuses were organised by central government to provide standardised statistics on population; tithe apportionments were part of a national movement to rationalise clerical incomes, by ensuring that money-rents everywhere replaced payments in kind; directories were commercial attempts to sell useful information to the principal inhabitants of local towns and villages. Therefore evidence drawn from these sources varies in range, depth, reliability and levels of involvement with the subjects described. Yet out of this puzzling mixture of statements and statistics the historian has to reconstruct, as best he can, what local communities were like.

Where points of contact exist, we are naturally keen to discover how far sources seem compatible and mutually supporting, and how far they are discordant. This is not to isolate some documents as 'true' and others as 'false': we are embarked on a far more subtle and hazardous process than that. Our interpretation will certainly be more complicated than if we had used only one source, but at the same time it will be a more realistic reflection of the convoluted truth. *In our minds we allow documents to adjust to each other, so that we become increasingly conscious of their relative strengths and weaknesses, and can begin to construct an overall picture.* Census enumerations, for example, give us information about every man, woman and child in a given locality (names, relationships, ages, occupations and birthplaces), but they can be misleading about certain family relationships or the occupations followed by wives and children. They will describe some men as farmers, and even mention their total acreages and the number of men and boys they employed, but they will not reveal where each man's land lay. By contrast, a tithe apportionment with its map will show who owned and who tenanted every field in the parish. In its turn, however,

---

[1] E. A. Wrigley, 'Family Limitation in Pre-Industrial England', *Economic Hist. Rev.*, 2nd ser., xix (1966), 82-109.

it may be quite vague about the number of tenants in a tightly built-up area and precisely which cottages or tenements they occupied.

In spite of such difficulties, these two kinds of source are often compared and interwoven, especially when they are close in date. For example, they underpin the technique of 'house repopulation' which is used to discover where individuals and families lived in 19th-century settlements. In other words, the strongly topographical evidence of tithe apportionments is deliberately put against the much more personal detail of census returns.[1] The normal point of contact between the sources lies in personal names: the head of a family mentioned by a census enumerator may be repeated in a list of owners or tenants in the apportionment. Once links have been made, it may be possible to see not only where families lived and where they held land, but where particular classes, occupations and even ethnic groups tended to congregate, and what living conditions were like in particular streets and houses.

One of the fascinations of local history is that it often gives the opportunity of using non-verbal evidence — such as domestic buildings, churches, funerary monuments, tools and implements, archaeological sites, field-systems, industrial remains and a host of other landscape features. For example, several years ago I was thrilled to find that an attractive green lane along our parish boundary, now merely a farm-track noted for prolific cowslips, was described in a 16th-century manorial survey as 'The Quenes High Waye' leading to a market town ten miles away. It is in fact part of a broad drove-road which for centuries linked two different but interdependent agricultural regions. But exciting though this kind of co-ordination can be, it often raises new problems.

Words and physical remains are very different kinds of historical evidence, and sometimes they appear to conflict. They therefore have to be carefully studied, each in its own terms, before they can be convincingly associated. Generally these apparent contradictions disappear when we realise that we have wrongly or inadequately interpreted one or both kinds of evidence. Let me give a simple example. In 1860 a Suffolk parson named Richard Cobbold wrote of his rectory, 'I built this house in the year 1827'. An inspection of the surviving building soon reveals a substantial timber-framed structure dating from the 16th or 17th centuries, to which a large brick wing had been added in the early 19th century! The building therefore has a far more complicated structural history than Cobbold's rather loose language suggests. The written statement, however, did reveal his personal attitude to the old-fashioned parsonage which he had inherited, and thought beneath his dignity. This, in a minor way, is the sort of problem and opportunity which Barrie Trinder had in mind when he wrote of historical and archaeological evidence coming 'fruitfully into conflict'.[2]

---

[1] A. Henstock, 'House Repopulation from the Census Returns of 1841 and 1851', *LPS,* 10 (Spring 1973), 37-52.
[2] B. Trinder in A. Rogers & T. Rowley (eds), *Landscapes and Documents* (1974), p. 79.

7. CREATIVE INTERPRETATION

Records, like the little children of long ago, only speak when they are spoken to, and they will not talk to strangers.
(C. R. Cheney, *Medieval Texts and Studies*, 1973, 8)

At this point an especially venomous nettle has to be grasped. How does the historian undertake his most demanding and creative task, which is to shape his own interpretation of the past? What is happening in our brains as we try to formulate our overall conclusions, and gird ourselves for the demanding business of writing? Of course it is true that an alarming number of people are content to guess and 'make up' their history. Evidence does not bother them, for they inhabit a technicolour and perfumed realm of unfettered imagination. Others approach history as mere collectors, assembling and pasting together snippets of information without any attempt to analyse or synthesise them. Real historians, however, are intellectually and morally bound to penetrate the past in a much more thoughtful and painstaking way.

As was discussed in the last chapter, our first objective must be to 'argue' with our documents and other evidence, until we have a satisfying picture of their combined significance. The result is a mass of factual and judgmental knowledge, which is the essential basis for broader interpretation. It may seem dangerous to assert that we are also, as we ponder our evidence, using imagination. Of course this does not mean that at a certain point we cut loose and romance wildly. In fact, imagination is only used as a way of of breathing life into historical 'facts' and extending the scope of our critical faculties. It is, frankly, a form of speculation but *only* on the basis of known evidence. At the same time we confess our ignorance, by pointing out what sources do *not* say, what is unknown about the past and what, nevertheless, may have happened — though no evidence can be found to prove or disprove it.

But historical interpretation involves more than detailed attention to sources, vital though that is. Pieces of evidence are merely raw materials which the historian controls and uses for his own creative purposes, and they recede in importance as an over-arching reconstruction begins to crystallise in the mind. The emphasis is now on one's *own* vision of the past and how it relates to existing historical knowledge: not only describing what is known about a particular subject, but trying simultaneously to explain its wider significance. The task is undeniably difficult and time-consuming, for one's interpretation has to be in the form of a logical and systematic debate, full of ideas, questions, uncertainties and judgements. Moreover, one's views may take some time to settle down, and even while writing one may still be refining the argument.

It cannot be said too often that good history, whether spoken or written, has shape, purpose and direction. Because it has been logically designed, it is not choked with masses of ill-digested fact and quotation. Many bits of evidence and opinion will have been considered, but only as the raw material for broader statements or judgements. Some factual detail will of course appear in our interpretation, but only to substantiate historical points and to sustain particular arguments. In other words, proper historians, though they are always thinking about evidence and sometimes quoting directly from it, are always trying to 'see the wood for the trees'. Their basic intention is make connections, to clarify, generalise and draw conclusions.[1]

Vital to the shaping of our interpretations is the realisation that historical work is provisional and cumulative, never final and definitive. While doing research we obviously hope that our discoveries will be of interest and value to others (otherwise we would not want to publish). The converse is that we cannot ignore what other historians say and write. They can teach us about new sources and techniques, and offer studies which compare with our own. More importantly, they bring us into contact with a range of priorities, standards, opinions and arguments, and remind us of those general concepts, models and theories which lie behind all serious research. Consider, for example, the great interest today in family and community history. This is an emphasis which arises from both academic research and popular interest, and its influence has filtered through to almost every other form of history. Whatever our chosen subjects, we are now much more conscious of the structure of families, the importance of kinship, the extent to which people moved house and job, the extent to which others 'stayed put', variable expectations of life, the amount of child mortality and illegitimacy, the effect of birth control, the prevalence of re-marriage, and many other issues. In other words, ideas have the habit of spreading from one field of endeavour to another and, in so doing, they stimulate new thinking, new research and frequent re-assessment.

It is therefore a crude simplification to regard history as the creation of solitary researchers, entombed in silent libraries, book-lined studies and record offices. Of course in one sense historical research *is* a lonely business (far more so than, for example, the pursuit of archaeology or architectural history), but a good piece of history is the brainchild of someone who has deliberately sought contact with other minds — by means of conversation, correspondence and, above all, reading. *An historian who ignores the work of other toilers in the same and related fields, is bound to be crippling his own appreciation of the past.* No matter what the subject, we should always try to measure our discoveries against current historical opinion, to see how far they

---

[1] To generalise does not mean to over-simplify, for nothing must be deceitfully omitted which is inconvenient or contradictory to one's case.

might confirm, amplify, modify or contradict that opinion. That is why, at the start of our writing, we usually refer to other people's work, trying to move logically from the known to the unknown. It is also why, as we later develop our own detailed arguments, we still repeatedly refer in both text and notes to what others have put into print.

Of course the process of interpretation will have begun long before writing is seriously contemplated. While evidence is being found and analysed, one will already be thinking of possible uses and lines of argument. However, to get one's historical opinions into anything resembling a final shape, it always helps to communicate with others. One way of clarifying the mind, for instance, is to prepare a short talk or lecture. A much more effective way, without any doubt, is to commit oneself to writing.

To end this rather theoretical discussion, and to turn our minds towards the practical demands of writing, let me quote a specific example of interpretation taken from Gwyneth Nair's book on the parish of Highley in Shropshire:

> In 1793, farm labourers in Highley were paid 8d a day plus their keep.* In addition, most of them kept a pig, which had replaced the cow as the poor man's only stock. Four shillings a week, with or without meals, was a very poor wage, and inflation forced it up, though probably not in line with rising prices. By 1803, Plymley assessed the average agricultural worker's wages in Shropshire at seven shillings a week rising to nine shillings during harvest.* This was below the national average of 10 shillings a week estimated by Burnett.* Agricultural wages continued to rise (if less quickly than prices) during the Napoleonic Wars: in Highley there was the added stimulus of alternative industrial employment. In addition, some labourers had large gardens whose produce could supplement the family diet. Their wives and children, too, could add to the family income by part-time work. In September 1827, for example, the wife of Richard Dodd, a labourer, spent the whole day 'leasing' (gleaning) and returned home only at 7 p.m.*
>
> Even so, agricultural labourers and their families lived in relative poverty for much of their life-cycle: the young couple had children who could not yet contribute to the family income; the older man could find his wage cut as infirmity, especially the rheumatism which particularly affected farm workers, curtailed his ability to work. Labourers were not able to retire, and had to work as long as their health permitted: in the census returns there are several labourers aged between 70 and 78.[1]

In two short paragraphs this writer has deployed the work of other historians, quoted detailed evidence, analysed it, debated its significance, and drawn conclusions. She has remained clearly in control of her own knowledge, and imposed her own thinking on the subject — creating her own objective yet personal interpretation which nobody else could duplicate. This is history.

---

[1] G. Nair, *Highley: The Development of a Community, 1550-1880* (Basil Blackwell, 1988), pp. 181-2. The asterisks show where references were appended in the original text.

8. STARTING TO WRITE

There are three parties ... to the process of interpretation: the interpreter, the mind he interprets, and the mind to whom he interprets.
(A. E. Levett, *Studies in Manorial History*, 1938, p. 8)

Historical writing is essential to historical understanding, and those who shrink from undertaking it are something less than historians.
(J. Tosh, *The Pursuit of History*, 1984, p. 94)

Do not postpone writing for too long because it can so easily be for ever. Some people procrastinate by saying that they have not finished their research, but this is an excuse rather than an explanation. Of course one's evidence never seems enough in quantity or quality, and no research is ever definitive for all time. Indeed, one may sometimes change one's mind and come to different conclusions on certain points. There is no disgrace in that, for the search for historical truth demands honesty and open minded-ness, and it never ends. Similarly the hunt for background reading to illuminate what one is finding locally, and for studies which are comparative to one's own, is also never-ending. Yet beyond a certain stage one's approach is not likely to alter signific-antly, and one should take the plunge. The longer writing is delayed, the more difficult it becomes to find motivation and to organise a formidable mass of material. As R. H. Worth said, 'One always writes too soon; but if one puts it off, one may not write at all'.[1] Or, as an extra-mural student once put it to me with quiet fatalism, 'It's a race with mortality'. In practice one does not necessarily have to write the whole study consecutively from A to Z: small sections of text, dealing with distinct aspects of the total subject, can be written separately and incorporated later into the larger work.

Before one begins to write a text, even in note form, two kinds of strategic pre-planning are highly desirable. First, thought should be given to the logical framework around which every satisfying piece of history must be built. Whether a book, dissertation, article or short note, it should contain the following elements, in roughly this order:

    1. A clear statement of the basic subject, or problem, to be investigated.

---

[1] H. P. R. Finberg quoting R. H. Worth in J. Thirsk (ed.), *Agrarian History of England and Wales*, iv (1967), vii.

2. Some discussion of the context of that subject, which is
   a) *geographical* or *topographical*, because one usually needs to depict the place or area where the human drama took place, and
   b) *historiographical*, because new work should be related to the publications of other historians, both past and present. In this way, one shows the cumulative and reactive nature of research.
3. An explanation of the evidence and methodology which are used.
4. Forming the greater part of the piece, a detailed 'development' of the subject, breaking it down into its constituent parts, analysing a volume of varied evidence, and presenting an interpretation.
5. Lastly, a summary which highlights the broad conclusions.[1]

(In Appendix 10, pp. 118-20, a published article is dissected to emphasise the importance of such a broad, logical structure).

Secondly, one's subject has to be divided into manageable, reasonably self-contained lengths. A book, as everyone knows, is normally divided into chapters; it may also have major 'parts' grouping chapters, and sub-sections within chapters. All these divisions usually carry separate titles. Shorter works like articles or pamphlets generally have sub-headings, or simply numbered sections. Three principal ways of dividing texts are observable in historical literature. The first, frequently seen in older parish histories, is by *period* or *royal dynasty* such as 'Before the Norman Conquest', 'The Tudor Period' and 'The Nineteenth Century'.[2] The second is by *subject*, for example 'Population', 'Earning a Living' and 'Recreation'.[3] The third and most common approach, however, is to interweave themes and chronology in a more subtle and realistic manner. For example, a history of Todmorden (Yorks.) published in 1996 contains chapters with titles such as 'Medieval Todmorden', 'The Rise of the Yeoman-Clothier', 'The Early Development of Textile Mills', 'Co-operation and Self-help' and 'Todmorden between the Wars'.[4] This mixture of themes and periods often seems the best approach, and is almost inevitable at the 'modern' end of history (after, say, 1750). But in whatever way you divide your subject, you will find awkward overlaps which demand cross-references and minor repeats.

---

[1] A very useful way of getting the measure of any piece of history, is to read the conclusions first!
[2] For example, M. K. Ashby's *Changing English Village* (1974) follows this course, though her chapters are subdivided into thematic sections with their own titles.
[3] David Iredale in his *Local History Research and Writing* (1974) recommended the following thematic headings: Lie of the Land, Settlement, Population, Work, Transport, Property, Government, Social Welfare, Education, Law and Order, Society, Religion and Recreation. However, it would be wrong to impose such a framework on all subjects and types of evidence.
[4] M. & F. Heywood & B. Jennings, *A History of Todmorden* (Smith Settle, 1996). In his *Fiery Blades of Hallamshire* (1991), David Hey devised an unusually complicated structure of three major parts which contained six sections and twenty-two sub-sections, all with separate and largely thematic titles.

PRELIMINARY PLANNING AND THE FIRST DRAFT

Before tackling any particular chapter or section, one should re-assemble all relevant information — whether in the form of slips, cards, transcripts, facsimiles, print-outs, notes from secondary reading, analyses, indexes or whatever. I find it immensely helpful to spread these things out physically, on a large table or on the floor. For increasing numbers of people, this stage will involve the shuffling of disks and the printing-out of hard copies (which are much easier to study than any text on a screen). The mere act of finding and re-reading all these bits of evidence helps to clarify their relative significance, and may lead to the rejection of inessential items. Furthermore, while the raw materials are spread out, one can experiment, for as long as it takes, with their physical arrangement, in the hope of finding a satisfying sequence which can form the basis of a piece of writing.

With all the evidence fresh in the mind, and already to some extent ordered, we are in a position to rough out a preliminary 'skeleton' or outline plan which can later be expanded into continuous prose. The purpose is not merely to condense bits of evidence which seem important, but to establish the main twists and turns of an historical argument. The actual length of these vital notes is a matter of personal choice and experience. While some fluent and practised writers do no more than jot down the principal ideas behind a whole chapter, most people will probably prefer a more detailed approach — at least sketching the nub of each successive paragraph (Appendix 11, pp. 121-2). It is important to realise that these notes are not a sacrosanct blueprint but a stimulus to get our thoughts moving: we may have several attempts at producing a satisfying plan, and even then the final version may not be slavishly followed as we write.[1]

The outline plan provides the raw material for writing the first draft. While the ideas flow, write quickly and be thankful. If you are writing long-hand, be sure to leave plenty of space between lines, because sooner or later you will want to make alterations. The great advantage of a modern word-processor is that one can alter the text very easily, and all the unwanted 'garbage' immediately disappears. At this drafting stage, however, it is vitally important that you do not torment yourself with niceties of style and grammar. Nor should you spend a long time trying to compose a perfect first paragraph. Many experienced writers say that in their first draft they bang out anything which comes into their heads in order to get the prose moving! *Above all, do not fall for the temptation of stopping every few minutes and reading over what you have just written.*[2] This may occasionally be useful to confirm a train of thought, but can easily become a sort of nervous paralysis which seriously delays progress. At all costs keep the text moving and — in spite of the temptation — do

---

[1] Interestingly, most people choose to write this plan in longhand rather than on the word-processor.
[2] The same point applies to the word-processor. One may be tempted to scroll back regularly to re-read one's text far too frequently, or to print-out with extravagant frequency.

not get bogged down with every piece of fine detail. Writing quickly, especially on a word-processor, you may produce very inflated, repetitive prose, or you may miss out parts of the argument and slide over complications. These defects do not matter because they can be repaired later.

As a way of getting one's thoughts moving again, it certainly pays to re-read (and perhaps revise) what was written the day before. W. G. Hoskins advised that a writer should leave off a day's work 'without completely exhausting the subject in hand'.[1] The next day he can pick up the threads with far less trouble than if beginning a totally new subject. However, it has to be remembered that although professional authors can sit down to the task almost daily, many part-timers have to write intermittently in spare moments. In that case, it is important to write at fairly regular intervals (at least once a week) rather than in widely-spaced bursts of activity. On each occasion one needs a minimum of several hours to make real progress. The odd half-hour is not enough to get the creative juices working.[2]

In spite of this emphasis on the value of regular writing, one major exception must be conceded. If it proves difficult to write on a particular topic, one should temporarily abandon the attempt — certainly for several days — and then return with a fresh mind. By this strategy the solution is often found which at first seemed so elusive.

If you are writing long-hand, it is advisable to use only one side of the paper — in case you want to do any cutting and pasting at a later stage. Also, remember to number your pages as you write, or you will be in a muddle by the day's end. The same point applies when you print pages from a word-processor, for they too must be numbered. While notes and transcripts are still available, it is also advisable to put in as many references as possible. If the details for a reference are not to hand, however, leave a gap which can be filled later, and do not break that precious flow of thought and effort.

Try to make sure, even at this early stage, that each paragraph is reasonably self-contained and built around the making and development of one major point. Skilled writers usually convey their gist in a key sentence near, or at, the beginning of each paragraph — thus stating the point early and clearly (Appendix 19, No.7, pp. 145-6). It is also important that each paragraph connects logically with its neighbours, and thus appears part of an organised discussion. In practice this means using words and phrases which crucially point backwards and forwards, such as 'Another strong trend in this period ...' and 'An even worse tragedy was about to happen'. Sure signs of sloppy writing are overlong, rambling paragraphs which have no obvious shape or core of ideas. *If a printed page has no paragraph-break in it, you can be sure that*

---

[1] W. G. Hoskins, *Local History in England* (3rd edn, 1984), p. 227.
[2] I have long admired authors who habitually rise early and begin the day by writing for a few hours, but am not one of them!

it will be difficult to read. Equally suspect are very short paragraphs consisting of single sentences, because they avoid discussion and are merely a form of listing. (For examples of good and bad paragraphing, see pp. 128-31, 143-6.)

The shape of this book has probably given the impression of a linear system in which one clear-cut stage succeeds another. *In real life, however, research and writing regularly overlap.* Ideas are sometimes written up while evidence is being studied, and are later slotted into the main text. On the other hand, historians in the midst of writing are often driven back to their documents because new questions arise or because the coverage is in some way unsatisfying. Moreover, documents have an irritating habit of turning up late in the day, and this too can lead to heart-searching revision.[1] In practice therefore, you may experience a constant interplay between your work on sources, your reading of other historians, and your actual writing.

SOME GUIDELINES FOR WRITING

When one is writing history, three important and well-recognised 'modes' should be kept in balance. *Description* conveys an event or scene at a particular time; *narrative* gives the sequence of events and emphasises time and change; and *analysis* is the attempt to explain why things happened, and to show how events were connected.[2] Every student of history has to learn not to write long passages of description or narrative, and then as an afterthought insert small pieces of analysis. He must keep all three dimensions in regular play, as the past is both surveyed and explained. Other kinds of balance must be preserved as well: the reader should be moved frequently, backwards and forwards, between detail and broad generalisation, between facts and judgements, between the locality and the wider world (Appendix 19, pp. 139-50).

Another important device is *comparison*. Thus, in describing how a town was governed in the 17th century, we may profitably compare it with other towns of the period, or compare it with the same town in earlier and later centuries. This kind of movement through time and space not only gives life to a text, but helps to measure the significance of what is being studied. The need to compare, and to place work in a wider framework, explains the frequent use of 'general' sources like lay subsidies, hearth-tax returns, poll books, returns of expenditure on the poor, and census abstracts. Their great virtue, apart from the fact that they are often in published form, is that they survey whole areas or counties, at one time and in a reasonably

---

[1] Margaret Spufford has described 'the historian's ultimate nightmare'. After her book on late-17th century Eccleshall was finished, a highly relevant stray document came to light. It necessitated the writing of a special postscript: M. Spufford, *Poverty Portrayed* (1995), pp. 69-70. Sometimes delays in publishing mean that material is outdated before it appears: see J. Haslam, *Anglo-Saxon Towns of Southern England* (1984), pp. ix, 356.

[2] G. R. Elton, *The Practice of History* (1984), p. 118; A. Marwick, *The Nature of History* (3rd ed., 1989), ch. 6, 'The Historian at Work: The Writing of History'.

consistent manner. Therefore they enable the historian to judge local communities *relative to each other* (Appendices 1 & 6, pp. 90-3, 107-10). Furthermore, other historians have probably used these sources already and drawn conclusions from them, which gives even further scope for comparison.

The ultimate aim in writing is to design an unbroken chain of systematic argument, which not only describes what happened in the past but almost simultaneously tries to explain why it happened. This can only be done when the evidence has been wholly assimilated, and when the logic of an historical interpretation has been thoroughly worked out. What we write is also truly personal and unique, and can never be repeated by another writer, or even by ourselves at a different age. This duality, a blend of the objective and personal, makes the historian's task a particularly fascinating and demanding one. Ironically, while many of us are reluctant to start writing, we then spend insufficient time on the job and publish too soon!

Nobody can give a detailed formula for writing history, because in the last analysis good style can take different forms and is a reflection of individual personality. However, a few general principles can be hazarded.

Shaping the Past

Writing in 1691, in his 'Perambulation of Surrey', John Aubrey proudly described his research method as follows: 'I now set things down tumultuarily, as if tumbled out of a sack, as they came to my hand'.[1] Since then, legions of historians have copied Aubrey and written 'tumultuarily'. This is the kind of history which Joseph Hunter, the 19th-century Yorkshire historian, brilliantly described as 'a succession of facts detached, a rope of sand'.[2] Proper history, by contrast, must involve the leaven of ideas, judgement and discussion. *We must give shape to the past, and not present mere catalogues of miscellaneous facts, trivial anecdotes and lumps from original sources.* Nor must we drop slabs of national history into the story of local life, inadequately related to it. As Marshall has warned, 'The local historian is only drowned in information if he or she has no ideas to act as life-saving equipment'.[3]

The shorter the study, the more selective it should be, and the more difficult it is to write (see p. 29). It does not follow that we should only write about the unusual or the dramatic, such as royal visits, fatal accidents and those wretched murders which feature prominently in many local histories.[4] Murders may actually be of some importance, but only when they are embedded in a wider study of crime, law or morality. In a balanced account, we must also stress the typical and the ordinary.

---

[1] J. Aubrey, *A Perambulation of the County of Surrey*, vol. 1 (London, 1718), foreword 'To the Reader'.
[2] Quoted in Thomas Helsby (ed.), George Ormerod's *History of the County Palatine and City of Chester*, p.xi, vol.1 of the 2nd [revised] edn (1882).
[3] Marshall, *Tyranny of the Discrete*, p. 29.
[4] Another temptation is to dwell on famous sons and daughters who spent most of their lives elsewhere. Many older parish histories are full of such 'worthiness' and hagiography.

Indeed the regularities and slow-moving trends of life (the *longue durée*, to quote a fashionable phrase) are usually more important than isolated events.

Unfortunately many local historians do not exercise sufficient control over their evidence. They dutifully but unimaginatively summarise each document in turn, and thus allow the sources to shape their thinking. To write well, the historian must remain firmly in charge and draw out the evidence which suits his own critical purpose. At times this may, indeed, mean bringing certain documents under very close scrutiny, especially when they present problems of meaning and interpretation. Usually, however, the evidence is kept at greater distance as we survey clusters of miscellaneous sources, and use only those parts which seem telling and relevant to the case being presented.

Asking Questions

As with the analysis of documents, the best way of giving shape to writing is to pose intelligent questions. How many people lived there? Was the population rising or falling? How did people earn their living? Were there marked differences of wealth? How did the community govern itself? Primary enquiries of this kind lead to others of a more detailed nature. Here, for example, are ways in which Alan Rogers suggested that a local historian might probe the subject of religion:

> ... how important was religion among the community? How widespread was its acceptance? What proportion of the population was among the active or its more formal adherents? ... What religious organisations did they enjoy? When and how did they originate? And what were their relations, the one to the other? What sort of persons predominated within each organisation? And ... what sort of activity did they engage in? Were they inward looking or 'full of good works'? What attempts did they make to deal with the problems of their contemporary society, to reach those outside?[1]

In a piece of published history, such questions need not be stated overtly. Normally, in fact, they are not.[2] *The real value of an historian's questions is that they guide his thoughts as he ponders his evidence and writes. As a consequence, his text will contain strong threads of logic and order, of analysis and discussion.*

Confessing Doubt

Given the patchy and uneven nature of historical evidence, our knowledge of the past must always contain uncertainties, doubts and gaps. These must be acknowledged with candour. *Good written history is liberally sprinkled with actual or implied questionmarks, because the historian can never expect to uncover the whole truth.* In other words, there are always more questions than answers! The related issue of what kind of

---

[1] A. Rogers, *Approaches to Local History* (2nd ed., 1977), pp. 127-8.
[2] *Rhetorical* questions can be effective in historical writing, but only if used sparingly.

language should be used to express complicated judgements and degrees of possibility and probability, is discussed in Appendix 13 (p. 124).

Controlling Detail

The historian must not bombard the reader with details, but select those which best illustrate his argument. In other words, he must always make detail count by explaining its relevance. By doing this he escapes, as Lionel Munby once expressed it, from 'the prison of his own knowledge'.[1] *Selection also implies rejection; you cannot expect to use all your evidence in writing, however painfully it was gathered or joyfully found.* Although an historical interpretation should be based on all relevant evidence, many facts and references will turn out to be inessential. On the other hand, you must certainly not suppress any evidence which is inconvenient or contradictory to your case — that would be intellectually dishonest. Chris Lewis's assessment of W. G. Hoskins summarises the importance of controlling detail :

> his strengths as a local historian, which should be a model for all, are precisely the ability to sum up the general development of a particular place without getting bogged down in the mire of detail, and then go on to show how the lessons of one place could be applied to others and to English history generally.[2]

Mastering Chronology

As has been said, a strong chronological thread must run through any piece of historical writing, because history records the passage of time and is concerned with those two precious themes of 'continuity' and 'change'. Indeed passages of pure narrative frequently introduce events in strict chronological order. Nevertheless, *time must not become a straight-jacket to the design of an historical argument. It is sometimes more effective, both for historical and literary reasons, to move around chronologically.* Many a biography, for example, begins with the death or funeral. Similarly most investigations of local riots and civil unrest begin by describing the event, and then move backwards to investigate its antecedents and causes.

The mention of a date is often of critical importance in understanding the full significance of a statement or judgement. Therefore it is good policy, in most circumstances, to mention dates at, or close to, the beginning of sentences, rather than at the end where they may lose impact, or give the reader a surprise.[3] Also be careful to bring together all phrases implying time.[4]

---

[1] L. Munby, review in *TLH*, 13, 4 (1978), 240.
[2] C. Lewis, *Particular Places*, p. 45.
[3] Do not, however, begin a sentence with a raw date. The little word 'in' demands to be used in this context. Instead of '1873 saw a declaration against Sacramental Confession receiving the assent ...', write 'In 1873 a declaration ...'
[4] Instead of 'A few months after her excommunication, Abigail died in 1639 and was buried in the churchyard of Thorpe', one would do better to write 'In 1639, a few months after her excommunication, Abigail died ...'

Polishing Quotations

Quotations, either from original sources or from the work of other historians, can be a highly effective device in writing because they introduce different, fresh voices. They must be long enough to make a telling point, but not so long as to bore the reader and unbalance the text. Many writers use excessively long quotations (Appendix 16, pp. 130-1). Presumably they do this in the hope of giving authenticity to their work, but in fact they merely expose their own inadequacies. In Finberg's words, 'there is no better way of unnerving the average reader at the outset than to hurl a chunk of Domesday at him, without any explanation of its terminology or so much as a hint that scholars are not altogether certain what some of the entries mean'.[1] Yet (it is worth saying again) *the crude stitching together of extracts from original sources is the most common mistake in the writing of local history.* Quotations can greatly improve the texture of historical writing, but they must be used judiciously and, like jewels in a crown, must be securely embedded in a text which debates and explains them. Needless to say, all quotations should be fully and accurately referenced. It is unethical, and indeed insulting, to use the words or ideas of somebody else — whether living or dead — without giving due acknowledgement.

Writing Humanely

Above all, one must try to produce history which is humane in both content and style. The central concern must be with people — thinking, sentient human beings in all their diversity. Unfortunately, many sources are primarily concerned with legal and administrative matters, and reveal little about human opinions, beliefs and emotions. Nevertheless, by working in a detached yet sympathetic way, the historian must get as close as he can to reconstructing what it felt like to be alive at that time. Even though one's writing will inevitably mention sources, methods of analysis, statistics and the physical world, these ought never to be regarded as ends in themselves but as merely contributing to the complex story of man.

Yet the opposite is frequently the case. As John Marshall once remarked, 'Plenty of people have written about the Poor Law, but very few, convincingly, about the poor!' Similarly economic, architectural and landscape historians have frequently written in a totally descriptive, de-humanised and soulless way. Timber-framed buildings, for example, or the earthworks of a shrunken village, have no historical value in themselves, unless they are explained as an expression of human thoughts and actions. Again, prices are not simply statistics: they show the value which people put on commodities, a value which the historian's language should reflect. In the study of local history, we are usually thinking about ordinary, relatively obscure and 'unsung' people and trying, with compassion yet without sentimental gush, to

---

[1] H. P. R. Finberg in Finberg & Skipp, *Local History, Objective and Pursuit* (1967), p. 85.

reconstruct something of their lives. *The local historian has no greater reward than to be able to show that the lives of ordinary people had meaning and dignity; that they were individuals and certainly did not regard themselves as equals, socially or morally; that they, like the 'great' and 'famous', had hopes and fears, joys and pains, achievement and failure.*

Because of the nature of historical evidence we often concentrate on human groups, for example those who pursued the same occupation, had a common religious faith, or regarded themselves as belonging to the same social stratum, but we must also seize those rarer opportunities of writing about individual men, women and children. This does not mean throwing in every personal titbit we happen to know: simply that where we are able to say something of personal importance, we should express it with humanity and dignity. 'I am an historian', said Henri Pirenne, 'Therefore, I love life'.[1]

Avoiding Moral Superiority

Too many historians, with the benefit of hindsight, write from a predominantly modern perspective which presupposes that everything which happened in the past was quite inevitable. They adopt a superior tone over earlier generations, pitying them for their superstitions and prejudices, and unfairly blaming them for not seeing the full consequences of their actions. Worse still, they judge historical individuals and communities by the moral and intellectual standards of today, and make little attempt sympathetically to understand how it felt to be alive at a particular period, as events unfolded uncertainly and new problems arose without warning. What, for example, was it like to be an overseer of the poor in a period of growing unemployment and economic recession, caught between the increasing demands of desperate paupers and the complaints of angry rate-payers? Parallels with the present may be instructive, but our writing should have no place for condescension and moral superiority.

Revealing Background and Personality

As a person aiming to study the past objectively, the historian must certainly strive to keep his own beliefs and prejudices under control. On the other hand, his personality and contemporary involvements will inevitably influence what he writes, and he should not be afraid of revealing them. It is better to write one-sided and partial history, and to be frank about it, than to have a secret agenda or to try any form of deceitful indoctrination, political, religious or otherwise. When Edward Thompson wrote that 'Enclosure ... was a plain enough case of class robbery, played according to fair rules of property and law laid down by a parliament of property-owners and lawyers', he may not have achieved the highest standards of historical

---

[1] Marc Bloch, *The Historian's Craft* (Manchester UP, 1954), p. 43.

impartiality, but at least he was giving a useful and thought-provoking way of looking at a familiar problem.[1] However objective we try to be, our writing remains an expression of ourselves. It should therefore show individuality.

Because it was then thought entirely wrong to use words like 'I' or 'mine', some older academic historians relied heavily on the regal 'one' or on phrases like 'this present writer'. Another option was to employ passive tenses and impersonal constructions like 'It can be argued that ...' Now, however, the first person singular is seen more frequently and can be an effective way of emphasising history as a personal quest. This device should not be used too liberally, however, for it can easily give the impression of self-centredness and arrogance.

---

[1] E. P. Thompson, *The Making of the English Working Class* (Pelican, 1968), pp. 237-8.

9. PRODUCING A FINAL DRAFT

He comprehended his matters in short, quick and high sentences, eschewing prolixity, casting away the chaff of superfluity, and showing the picked grain of sentence ...
(Tribute to Chaucer, from Caxton's edition of *The Canterbury Tales*, c.1484)

No language has better ingredients than English; no language has ever been more monstrously ill-treated and deformed by vandals and incompetents.
(Kenneth Hudson, *Dictionary of Diseased English*, 1977, p. xiii)

Writing must not be regarded as a mere chore, a second-rate activity to be done in the odds and ends of one's time ...
(R. M. Robbins, *Antiquaries Jour.*, lxviii, pt 1, 1988, 5)

In second and later drafts, a writer is normally concerned with the refinement of prose so that it is lucid, coherent and elegant. Again, nobody can give a precise formula for success, but we can find plenty of examples which show what to aim at, and what to avoid.

REVISING AND RE-DRAFTING

Many of us using word-processors are continuously revising and tinkering as we write: this is a great advantage of the new technology. Nevertheless, when the first draft is finished, we must be prepared to revise it extensively. After all, it is usually possible to write the same statement in several fundamentally different ways (Appendix 12, p. 123). The number of revisions will vary from individual to individual, but most of us need several. Very rare is the writer who can produce a publishable draft at the first attempt, and anyone who claims that gift should be regarded with polite suspicion! Revision may mean changing the order of words, inserting new material, deleting unnecessary and overblown prose, or totally re-structuring whole paragraphs. When a passage has been re-thought and recast, it is important to check the surrounding prose for other necessary adjustments. *One major reason for the ugliness and confusion of much modern writing is an unwillingness to undertake careful revision.* 'Prose is like hair; it shines with combing.'[1]

---

[1] I cannot find the origin of this neat simile. It may be attributable to Gustave Flaubert.

EXPANDING AND CONDENSING

One is frequently dissatisfied with a passage, without knowing exactly what is wrong. This 'inner voice' of criticism should be heeded because it is invariably right. On maturer reflection, one realises that the logic of an argument has not been worked out thoroughly enough. Something may be missing, or an idea, though mentioned, may not have been given sufficient weight. A comment which began as a subordinate clause frequently has to be given the status of a separate sentence, or more. On the other hand, it is an even more common experience to have to prune.

In a first draft nearly all writers use unnecessary words, phrases, sentences and even paragraphs. For example, we often commit the sin of tautology by using two or more words which are identical or close in meaning, such as 'the inexperienced beginner'. It is also easy to leave behind more of our 'mental scaffolding' than is justifiable: 'Now we must turn, as in the last chapter, to the subject of ...' Or we may find that we have included facts and ideas which impede the flow of an argument and are better placed in footnotes or appendices. *The more compact our writing, the more forceful and effective it becomes.* We cannot afford to waste space as older antiquaries did with their more egotistical and ruminative styles (No. 31, p. 137). Pascal wisely said that if he had had more time, he would have written less.[1]

CHOOSING WORDS

In the hope, as they think, of giving their prose greater dignity, weight and academic acceptability, many writers complicate their message quite unnecessarily. They actually prefer the complex to the simple, the oblique to the direct, the pompous to the plain. They choose the rare word where a common one would serve better, and they observe Finberg's tongue-in-cheek rule 'never to use one word where you can possibly use four'.[2] To fall for these temptations shows a careless disregard for the reader. Heaven knows that historical truth is complicated enough without being further obscured by our choice of words.

Every writer of history has a duty to choose words which are as precise and concrete as possible. He should not use vague terms like 'the people' or 'progress' when it is usually possible to say which people he has in mind, and what kind of progress. He must also be wary of historical labels such as 'The Middle Ages' and 'capitalism' which can mean different things to different minds. Linguistically and stylistically the greatest difficulty arises when we have to express judgements and opinions — with which history abounds. That is why the literature is full of adverbs

---

[1] *Oxford Dictionary of Quotations* (4th edn, 1996), p. 507.
[2] H. P. R. Finberg, 'How not to write Local History' in Finberg & V. H. T. Skipp, *Local History: Objective and Pursuit* (1967), p. 85. See H. W. & F. G. Fowler, *The King's English* (1906) and *Modern English Usage* (1926; 3rd edn, 1996, ed. R. W. Burchfield) for good advice on the choice of words.

like 'perhaps' and 'probably', of adjectives like 'uncertain' and 'ambiguous', and of phrases like 'the evidence suggests ...' or 'on balance, it seems likely that ...' The use of numbers has certainly given more precision to historical writing, but our main tools are still words, and they have to be used as responsibly and accurately as possible. Indeed, as journals of demographic and economic history amply demonstrate, *we are now struggling with a new challenge today: that of developing a civilised literary style which will express the increasing numeracy of our interpretations.*

Sentences vary in length, and rightly so. It has recently been suggested, however, that their *average* length should be no more than fifteen to twenty words.[1] Whether or not this rule is seriously adopted, the underlying point is a good one. In the heat of composition we often draft sentences which are far too long, and loaded with subordinate clauses, participles, semi-colons and other clutter. When such agglomerations are re-thought and broken down into shorter sentences, the message can always be put across more economically and persuasively.[2] Remember that word-processors can count words, and warn us of stylistic and grammatical infelicities (for example, 'you have started nine of the last thirteen sentences with the word, I').

THE IMPORTANCE OF STYLE

Although not writing literature in the strict sense, an historian must always strive to write prose which is smooth, shapely and economical. To convey ideas unambiguously he must choose the minimum number of effective words, and think constantly about their arrangement — if necessary changing the word-order many times. For example, it is generally good practice to place the subject at or near the beginning of a sentence, and to keep subject and verb as close as possible. Another important consideration is to give prominence to the words which matter most. Frequently an important word is lost in heavy choking verbiage, or appears early in a sentence and is weakened by later qualifying clauses. Though not an invariable rule, it often helps to reorganise sentences so that salient words come towards the end, as a sort of climax.[3] Similarly, in giving a string of examples it can pay to keep the most effective until last ('but above all'). In this quest for better shape and flow, it can be very helpful to read one's work aloud, or slowly in the head as if publicly declaiming.[4]

---

[1] Martin Cutts, *The Plain English Guide* (Oxford, 1995), p. 11.

[2] Students writing dissertations often worry about a word-limit of, say, 20,000 words. In my experience, a fifth of the verbiage of early drafts can usually be pruned away, and sometimes considerably more.

[3] In this and the next sentence, for example, I have endeavoured to highlight 'climax' and 'last'. This does not contradict the point made earlier about the value of putting dates at the *beginning* of a sentence (above, p. 64).

[4] To pursue the musical metaphor further, one should avoid the jerky effect of too many short words in succession ('He put it out that at the time he could not come'), and the repetition of sounds when words begin with the same letter ('... barely been begun before ...').

A responsible writer must constantly seek opportunities for cutting, tightening and strengthening his prose. For example, when referring quite properly to the work of other historians, one should not clutter a text with titles of articles or books: those details normally appear in footnotes, endnotes and bibliographies. The text, with an appropriate reference number, may simply say, 'As James Smith has recently proved' or 'In Dr Smith's opinion'. More importantly, all writing should be carefully combed for sentences beginning with impersonal and unnecessary constructions like 'It can be argued that' or 'It should go without saying that', for weak clichés and inappropriate metaphors and similes,[1] and for colloquial expressions which make the language flabby and less direct. Perhaps the worst trap of all is 'there is', 'there are', 'there were', etc., which many people transfer unconsciously from speech to writing.[2] *We must be prepared to mould and re-mould our writing until it flows with ease and dignity, and until key words and phrases have the prominence and impact which they deserve.* In this sense, style is not an optional extra or a cosmetic: it is part of the basic craft of communicating with the widest possible readership.

AVOIDING JARGON

In his inaugural lecture at Leicester in 1966 William Hoskins drily observed, 'I once wrote a book with a simple title of *The Making of the English Landscape*, but I ought to have called it "The Morphogenesis of the Cultural Environment" to make the fullest impact'.[3] He would have chortled to hear that a new course on Garden History in an English university was recently re-named as 'Ornamental and Functional Space: The Aesthetics and Conceptuality of Horticultural Activity in Past Social Contexts'. In the *Oxford English Dictionary* one definition of the word 'jargon' is 'the cant of a class, sect, trade or profession'. It is, in other words, a terminology adopted by a specialised group to enable its members to communicate with each other. Deliberately or not, it has the simultaneous effect of deterring and excluding outsiders. Jargon is a curse in all academic disciplines, but is particularly reprehensible in the study of human society. Not only does it make wider communication difficult, but it frequently prevents us from thinking clearly in the first place. Examples of ugly jargon are regularly adopted or coined, usually by professionals who should know better. Indeed, historians in the van of the computing revolution are fast

---

[1] Metaphors and similes should be used sparingly in historical writing: they need careful consideration and must be entirely apt.

[2] This construction is not to be avoided at all costs; occasionally it can be the right choice for good literary reasons. My criticism applies to its thoughtless overuse, and the unwillingness to think of better and stronger verbs; see below, p. 73-4. Needless to say, ugly colloquial expressions like 'standards-wise' should be avoided entirely.

[3] W. G. Hoskins, *English Local History: The Past and the Future* (Leicester UP, 1966), p. 21.

developing their own brand of verbal fog and 'gobbledygook'. In recent years we have been asked to swallow:

- non-migratory mobility
- residential propinquity
- multi-source nominal record linkage
- commensality
- commodification
- prosopography

and many others.[1] It is no accident that those in the habit of using jargon are poor writers anyhow. The seductive power of fashionable words like 'function' and 'situation' can have similar deterrent and nonsensical effects. Thus, with all solemnity, one recent writer concluded that 'the main reason why so many parish registers were unreliable was probably a function of the system of registration'.

Nevertheless, a distinction should be made between jargon and technical language. Jargon is *unnecessarily* obscure language, often characterised by an ugly accumulation of nouns, written by members of specialised groups who have no interest in communicating with outsiders. By contrast, technical language derives from inescapably specialised areas of life (for example, industrial processes such as 'tawing', legal instruments such as 'recognizances', and theological concepts such as 'transubstantiation'). They are therefore perfectly acceptable in the writing of history providing they are explained when first used — either in the text or in a footnote or glossary. Another kind of technical language is adopted or coined by historians themselves, to cover concepts which they wish to investigate. Thus they legitimately refer to the 'cost of living index', to 'mean household size' and 'age at first marriage'.

THE ABUSE OF NOUNS

A useful characteristic of the English language is that two nouns can be put side by side. Phrases like 'income tax' and 'county town' are a concise form of expression where the first noun acts as an adjective. Unfortunately, this device is increasingly abused by a wide variety of writers, not least by journalists, bureaucrats and academics. Instead of using appropriate adjectives, participles and prepositions (particularly those vital little words, 'of' and 'for'), these new barbarians string nouns together with careless abandon — three, four, five or more in a row. They are not even capable of inserting the occasional hyphen or apostrophe, which might help the tortured reader. *Published history now teems with coarse and ponderous rows of nouns (perhaps*

---

[1] Commensality means 'eating together'. 'Commodification' appears to mean 'the increasing consumption of material goods, and its historical significance'. 'Prosopography' is very popular among ancient historians and medievalists: based on the Greek *prosopon* meaning 'face', it means the study of individual lives by putting together miscellaneous pieces of evidence, in other words, 'biographical notes' or 'notes on people'.

they should be called 'noun-strings') which make the language thick and obscure. One can invariably think of clearer, more logical and sometimes shorter ways of expressing the point. For example:

- birthplace location analysis (meaning 'the analysis of birthplaces')
- house plan classification types ('types of house-plan')
- volume analysis completion rate ('the rate at which volumes were completed')
- labour force participation rates ('the proportion of people at work')
- case fatality rate ('the proportion of those infected who died')
- wall painting condition audit ('survey of the condition of wall-paintings')
- census data capture sheet ('form for the analysis of censuses')
- Reader Information Services Department (proof that the disease has hit the PRO).

The fact that some nouns in this kind of writing are superfluous or actually mistaken, underlines its basic sloppiness. But the most obvious objection is that it distorts logic: the meaning of such strings does not dawn (if at all) until the *last* noun has been read. In languages with a more precise structure, for instance French or Latin, such clumsiness would be impossible and the word-order would be more logical, but in English we are witnessing the illiterate abuse of greater freedom.[1] Perhaps, at public expense, a warning system should be fitted inside all our brains: a bell should clang, or a red light wink, every time we write three or more nouns in a row![2]

PROMOTING VERBS

An undue stress on nouns leads to the devaluing of verbs, and therefore to a lumpy obliqueness in writing. After a few moments of self-criticism, a noun-laden phrase like 'in a period of acute population pressure and increasing conversion to arable' will come to life as, 'in a period when the population grew fast and ever more land was ploughed'. As Martin Cutts has recently advised, you should 'use the clearest, crispest, liveliest verb to express your thoughts'.[3] Yet, nowadays, many writers choose verbs which are passive and weak, such as 'is indicated', 'occurred' and 'has been found'. Furthermore they often place them at the ends of sentences, like a feeble death-rattle.

The devaluation of verbs advertises itself by two other regrettable habits. The first is the persistent use of abstract nouns such as 'factor', 'structure', 'pattern', 'activity', 'index' and, above all, 'situation'. It is not without significance that these

---

[1] Of course noun-strings are characteristic of the German language, and the habit appears to have seeped into Britain *via* America.

[2] One final, chilling example. An event in Durham's majestic cathedral in the year 2000 is advertised as 'The Durham Sacrament Sequence Project Performance'!

[3] Martin Cutts, *The Plain English Guide* (1995), p. 56.

words are usually embedded in noun-strings. The second habit concerns adverbs. They are of course a useful part of speech but can be overused in an effort to compensate, consciously or unconsciously, for the weakness of verbs.[1]

Great care should be taken with present and past participles. These can seriously unbalance sentences, when it would be better to make shorter statements or to use normal clauses with their own subjects. For example, 'In 1839 a new church was built, *having resulted* from a long campaign of money raising *lasting* several years and *organised* by a team of determined individuals'.[2] This stylistic habit is fairly general but particularly afflicts the more elderly among us. Of course, the worst possible misuse is the 'hanging participle' which creates straightforward nonsense: 'Having lost his capital, the estate was sold'.

THE FINAL REVISION

After you have written a passage, and got as close as possible to your final draft, put away the manuscript for a fortnight or more. On re-reading it, you will invariably spot imperfections which you had previously overlooked, such as:

- mistakes in spelling[3]
- inconsistencies in the use of numbers[4]
- mistakes in punctuation[5]
- the choice of wrong tenses, and the mixing of tenses[6]
- words which beg to be deleted[7]
- the old-fashioned use of capital letters with common nouns like Parish, Borough, Church and Overseer[8]

---

[1] For example, '.. becomes *effectively*'. In a more general sense, adverbs are often used too automatically. Why do we always have to *'readily* admit', *'fully* confess' and *'richly* deserve'? One should always comb one's prose for superfluous adverbs, and ensure that those which remain are apt and strong.

[2] The following wording is better. 'In 1839 a new church was built. The campaign to raise money lasted several years, and was organised by a team of determined individuals.'

[3] It is worth remembering that most spell-checks on computers will pass 'laud of the manner'! Among common errors are 'privelege', 'seperate', 'independant', 'benefitted' and 'fulfill'.

[4] Manuals vary in their advice about spelling out low numbers, unless in a sequence of quantities or statistics; some recommend up to one hundred, others to twenty or nine.

[5] While Victorian writers used too much punctuation, many modern writers do not use enough and think it trendy to do so. Commas in particular are underused. In references and bibliographies we see a dangerous tendency to omit stops and commas. Normally one should write 'In the seventeenth century', but 'in a seventeenth-century book'. When dealing with specific centuries, one can easily use hyphens inconsistently with the words 'early', 'mid' and 'late'.

[6] Mixing the present and past in the same sentence is a common mistake: 'In 1694 John had no more land to plough, but in 1697 he is actively seeking to expand the estate.' In general, one writes about the past in a past tense, but about surviving evidence in the present. Some writers frequently employ 'would have' and 'must have'; these are dangerous tenses which often show that the writer is guessing.

[7] For example, 'In spite of the fact that …' can be replaced by the single word 'Although …'

[8] This habit was very noticeable in Victorian times, and hangs over in higher age-groups. Americans are also prone to it. See A. F. Pollard, 'The Use and Abuse of Capital Letters', *Bulletin Inst. Historical Research*, v (1927-8), 1-12. Remember, however, that capital letters should be retained for special and specific usages like World War I and the New Poor Law.

- the ugly juxtaposition of two or more prepositions[1]
- the confusion of 'less' and 'fewer'[2]
- the careless use of deceptive adverbs like 'happily', 'frankly' and 'hopefully'[3]
- the loose spraying of 'it', a dangerous little word often used in different senses in the same sentence
- the overuse of 'the' which frequently retards the flow of writing when 'a', or no article at all, would be preferable.[4]

This is also the time to think about linking words such as 'furthermore' and 'nevertheless', or of words which give emphasis like 'indeed' and 'particularly'. Often we need to correct the order of words,[5] bring phrases together which imply time or place,[6] or make sure that we do not unnecessarily mix constructions in the same sentence.[7] At this stage too, one should check all references for errors and inconsistencies (see below, pp. 76-7).

All of us tend to overdo certain words, phrases and constructions (a god-send to analysts of literary style), but may not be conscious of them until we later re-read the text, or until someone else points them out. Fortunately the modern word-processor provides another way of spotting repetitions through its 'Find' key.[8] Usually it does not take long to think of alternatives or to remould the sentence.

Time should be found for checking the start and finish of one's creation, whether book, article or mere note. In their final form, the beginning and end of a piece need to be strong and preferably memorable, creating immediate interest in the one and offering a satisfying conclusion in the other (see examples on pp. 139, 150).

SEEKING CRITICISM

When a text is finished, and before it is published, it should be read by at least two other people — but do not be surprised if their reactions differ. One reader should be a specialist who has experience relevant to the subject, and another a non-specialist who will point out when the writing is unclear. It is sad that many historians, having sought help in the earlier stages of their research, publish their findings without seeking any further comment.

---

[1] For example, 'referred to in...'
[2] The correct use is 'less cheese' and 'fewer cheeses'.
[3] In a sentence like 'He was frankly an evil influence', the writer is being frank, not the evil person. Such misleading colloquialisms are best avoided in writing.
[4] Why, for example, do demographers refer so often to 'the' or 'a' plague when neither article is needed?
[5] 'He was one of seven invited people to the meeting.'
[6] 'In 1810 John Smith left £200 when he died.'
[7] 'Edward Brown left his tenement to his son Thomas, and his daughter Jane was to have £5.'
[8] Among my weaknesses is a tendency to overuse adverbs such as 'clearly','often' and 'increasingly'. A magnanimous friend of mine confesses that he overuses adjectives such as 'magnificent', 'superb' and 'outstanding'.

REFERENCES

Footnotes and endnotes are the normal kinds of reference, and are a vital part of the mechanism of history. They are not, as some people think, a form of masochistic generosity whereby we give away our best sources and hand a cudgel to our enemies. Nor are they a self-indulgent luxury, as some second-rate publishers assume. On the contrary, to give references is simply to declare one's good faith and to show that one has not invented the past. Because history is based on the interpretation of evidence, one must indicate the nature of that evidence and give readers the chance of consulting it for themselves. Not to do so is to invite suspicion and criticism; that is partly why much published local history is pooh-poohed by professionals.

Of course readers will treat references in very different ways. Some will ignore them altogether because they only want 'a good read'. Others may show interest in the occasional reference, as something worth following up. Those doing research in that or related subjects, however, will want to know the full range of sources behind a particular piece of writing, and may indeed want to consult some of the original manuscripts or secondary works for themselves. Because no piece of history can ever be 'the final word', references are therefore an invitation to keep the debate open and to take the work further. In this sense history is cumulative, though historians may 'co-operate' who work alone and never personally meet.

In giving references a balance must be struck. All quotations and all major facts and opinions, especially if they are important turning-points in the argument, must be supported by references. On the other hand, one's writing should not be over-burdened with great quantities of notes because that will simply deter and intimidate readers. For example, Eric Kerridge's seminal book on the *Agricultural Revolution* (1967) was famously marred by the number and length of its footnotes, which often occupied more space on the page than the text itself.

Three other points need to be remembered. First, several sources can be grouped into a single note — providing they have the same sequence as in the text, and do not take up too much space. Secondly, a manuscript or printed source should not be quoted unless it has been specifically consulted. If you have merely seen its mention elsewhere, the honest policy is to give one source as 'quoted in' the other. Lastly, while it is perfectly proper to supplement references with comment, and indeed to have notes consisting only of comment, you should not use this as an excuse for adding large chunks of extra text.

The traditional form of reference is the footnote which appears in smaller type at the bottom of the page. Its great advantage is that it is easily consulted when wanted. Similarly it is easily ignored. For about twenty years from the mid-1960s, however, endnotes (grouped at the end of each chapter, article or whole book) became much more common because they were set more easily by contemporary typists and printers; this method leaves the main text unbroken but causes the reader to flap pages in his search for a particular note. Finally, the rapid spread of word-processors since about 1980 has undoubtedly brought footnotes back into favour again. By this method one can easily add or delete notes at any stage of writing, and they are automatically re-numbered.[1]

In the text references should be indicated by a small discreet number — thus.[2] It should be placed, where possible, after the full-stop at the end of a sentence, but sometimes has to appear earlier, after a particular word or phrase. As a general rule, one should place the number *after* punctuation. In the case of footnotes, the sequence of numbers is usually by the page. With endnotes, however, one's sequence runs right through each chapter, article or whole book, and can therefore run into hundreds or thousands. To help readers find the appropriate information, endnotes should not only be clearly subdivided by chapter (each time giving the number and title), but every column should be headed by a further reference to relevant pages in the text.

The so-called 'Harvard' or 'Author-Date' system is a form of referencing used by many academics, including social scientists and archaeologists. Spectacularly unsuitable for historical writing, it creates ugly breaks in printed texts, for example (Razi & Smith, 1996, pp. 569-637), and cannot be adapted for primary sources. One particularly regrets that the Open University is wedded to this pretentious convention: it drills its students into a habit which they will have to 'unlearn' when they submit articles to the great majority of historical journals.[3]

Because references contain fine details such as initials and numbers, which are important in the search for books, articles and manuscripts, they must be accurate. Mistakes can easily creep in, especially when notes are being copied from one medium to another. Therefore, careful checking is essential when a final draft is being prepared, and again before final publication. Remember that, where bibliographies are included at the back of a book or article, footnotes or endnotes can be abbreviated: this is done on the assumption that the *full* details appear in the bibliography. (In Appendix 20, pp. 151-4, are rules recommended for references and bibliographies.)

APPENDICES

Where a writer judges that transcripts of documents and other background information would be of interest to the reader, but are too bulky for the main text, he may choose to use appendices. These are perfectly acceptable, providing they have relevance to the subject. If you have more than one appendix, make sure that they are numbered and listed on the contents-page. It would of course be wrong to put into appendices material such as tables, diagrams, maps and plates — these should be clearly labelled and integrated with the main text.[4]

---

[1] An argument can be mounted for retaining endnotes where references are very numerous. For example, H. R. T. Summerson's impressive book on *Medieval Carlisle* (2 vols, 1993) has a single chapter with no fewer than 2,386 endnotes.

[2] In the first edition of this book, reference numbers were placed in brackets. Being older and wiser, I would not do that again!

[3] How regrettable, too, that the Harvard system is used in Longman's Regional Histories.

[4] One might, however, put such items at the back if they are mentioned *in several parts* of the work.

10. PUBLISHING

Most historians choose *not* to publish their own work, and thereby avoid all the problems involved! They are content to submit articles to established journals and periodicals, or to write books commissioned by commercial or academic publishers.[1] As has been stressed before, the number of outlets is very large and still growing — although an approach does not necessarily lead to acceptance and one may have to tout one's manuscript around. On the other hand, a substantial number of local historians, as individuals and as societies, regularly publish their own work in forms ranging from leaflets to weighty books. These varied and increasingly attractive products are now frequently seen in bookshops, libraries, record offices, museums, information centres, conferences and fairs, and are a major advertisement for local studies.

If one decides to be one's own publisher, a host of practical, technical and financial possibilities present themselves. The most fundamental choice is whether to do a 'desk-top' job with one's own word-processor, or to seek a commercial printing firm. If one chooses a firm, they will normally be responsible for the type-setting, but money can be saved by supplying one's own 'camera-ready copy' (CRC) on disk. A local historian looking for a commercial printer should certainly 'shop around', for quotations can differ widely. One should ask for the cost of different quantities (e.g. 250, 500, 1000 copies), with and without CRC. If you are not supplying CRC, always ask to see final proofs. Increasingly, however, local historians are choosing to be their own printers and publishers, and are using relatively cheap programs for desk-top publishing (DTP).[2] The spread of digitalisation in the next few years will undoubtedly make home-publishing even more easy, attractive and cheap.

At a more detailed level decisions have to be made about type-face, layout, running heads, illustrations, type of cover, and binding. One has to decide whether to invite

---

[1] Nationally the two leading publishers of local history are Phillimore of Chichester (West Sussex) and Sutton Publishing of Stroud (Gloucestershire). All regions, however, have smaller commercial publishers who produce books on local history. Some universities (or their centres of local and regional history) also publish in this field.

[2] For a good introduction, see 'Desktop Publishing' and 'Word Processing' in *Writers' and Artists' Yearbook* (annually).

sponsors and advertisers to offset costs. Finally one has to ponder on the number of copies wanted, the intended price, and how the product is to be marketed. To settle these issues, one should certainly seek advice from more experienced authors as well as from commercial companies. To guide us through the technicalities of modern design, publishing and marketing, Bob Trubshaw's *How to Write and Publish Local History* (1999) is useful and timely. Here only a few general words of advice are needed:

1. Correct all proofs with the greatest care, using standard symbols.[1] Ensure consistency in your use of punctuation, numbers, sums of money, percentages, capital letters and other important details. Do a final check of your references, and make sure that they are in an acceptable standard form. (An astonishing number of writers and publishers make up their own referencing systems, as they go along.) When in doubt, consult the printed works of respected national publishers.

2. Do not use too complicated a title, for that will make you unpopular with librarians and bibliographers. It is often tempting to have a sub-title, generally after a colon, but this needs careful thought. Avoid the long verbose titles beloved of older antiquaries,[2] and 'clever' or pompous titles which often fall flat and date rapidly.[3] Make sure that the title on your cover is exactly the same as that on the title-page. (See no. 11 below, for titling the book's spine.)

3. Make sure your publication is dated on the title-page or on its reverse. It is amazing how many are not, which necessitates the use of 'no date' (nd) in bibliographies and references.

4. Obtain an ISBN (International Standard Book Number) from the following address: UK Standard Book Numbering Agency, 12 Dyott St, LONDON, WC1A 1DF. This will mean that your brainchild can be found by librarians, booksellers and readers, wherever they live.[4]

5. Include a contents-page listing every section in the book, with page numbers, and make sure that the details are accurate. Also, if necessary, add a List of Illustrations distinguishing categories such as Maps, Figures and Plates.

---

[1] See 'Correcting Proofs' in *Writers' and Artists' Yearbook*, which in turn is based on the advice of the British Standards Institute.

[2] For an extreme example: Charles Parkin, *A Reply to the Peevish, Weak and Malevolent Objections Brought by Dr Stukeley in his Origines Roystonianae, No. 2, … wherein the said Answer is maintained; Royston proved to be an old Saxon Town, its Derivation and Original; and the History of Lady Roisia shown to be a meer Fable and Figment* (Norwich, 1748).

[3] *An Elegant Place for All Seasons and All Mankind: Chipping Easton, 1810-50*. In this fictitious example, the sub-title should be the real title.

[4] See 'International Standard Book Numbering' in *Writers' and Artists' Yearbook*. The same section also gives advice about copyright libraries.

6. Maps can be very helpful, especially for readers who do not know the district. If you reproduce modern Ordnance Survey maps, permission has to be sought and a fee paid. It is better to draw your own maps concentrating on features mentioned in the text. Do not publish a scruffily drawn or hand-labelled map; it does not cost much to get your draft redrawn professionally. Computer mapping by means of a scanner is now increasingly feasible for non-experts.

7. Illustrations of any kind are welcome but must be strictly relevant to the text. Make sure that their significance is fully explained in carefully worded captions. One often sees historical photographs with feeble titles like 'The High Street long ago', graphs without proper headings, and tables with inadequate explanation of what their numbers and axes represent. One even sees figures and illustrations with no caption whatsoever. In fact, all illustrations should be self-explanatory and complete in themselves, so that they can be used independently (e.g. reproduced in other publications, or converted into transparencies for teaching). When you have two or more illustrations on a page, take care that each is clearly numbered and captioned: the text must be unambiguously adjacent to the relevant image. In trendy modern publications one is frequently confused by complicated layouts, by the unclear use of numbers, and by consolidated captions with silly formulae like 'clockwise from top left'.

8. Your publication should have good visual balance between black print and white space. Sometimes lines are spaced too far apart, but much more often pages are unpleasantly crammed with type. Many histories produced by private individuals and local printers look far too dense and crude, with childish over-large type, narrow margins and 'gutters', weak breaks between paragraphs, and an insufficient number of headings and sub-divisions. Particular attention must be paid to the spacing of CRC, because this influences the whole appearance of the printed page. For example, you have to decide how much space to leave at the end of each sentence. By leaving *two* spaces after the full-stop or reference number, which was the traditional rule for typists, you can certainly introduce more 'light and air'.[1]

9. Give thought to the type of paper to be used in your publication. You certainly want one thick enough to avoid 'show-through' from one face to the other. Many people choose glossy paper, which is better for the reproduction of plates. However, never forget that for normal print, and for black-and-white drawings, matt surfaces are much kinder on the eyes — especially under artificial light.

10. In a substantial book, the discerning reader deserves an index. You, as the writer, are best placed to do this job, though occasionally it can be entrusted to others. Sound,

---

[1] A generational argument is now being waged over this point. Younger people tend to prefer a single space after each sentence. Certainly, each colon and semi-colon should be followed by only one space.

if rather forbidding, guidance will be found in R. F. Hunnisett, *Indexing for Editors* (1977). Remember that an index should cover Persons, Places *and* Subjects (sometimes expressed as *Nominum, Locorum* and *Rerum*). The first two are often combined because they overlap, but the third is the most important, the most frequently omitted and the most difficult to achieve. In compiling a subject index, one frequently needs to devise key words which may not feature in the text itself, so that related subjects can be grouped under suitable headings (e.g. CATTLE with sub-headings like 'bullocks', 'bulls', 'calves' and 'heifers').

11. Much local history appears in the form of thin booklets stapled together or clamped by an untitled plastic spine. They can be economical to produce but unfortunately are easily mislaid — tending to become invisible on open shelves, and easily forgotten when put into box-files. It therefore pays, if you can manage it, to produce a publication which has a spine bearing the title (abbreviated if necessary). This calls for a minimum of about 60 pages. Make sure you use a binding which will not quickly fall apart!

12. If you produce a sizeable book, the printer's bill will run to several thousand pounds. Money-raising is best done by a team because it demands effort, persistence and planning. The normal methods include pre-publication subscriptions or loans, the finding of private and commercial sponsors, and grants from local authorities and private trusts.[1] The amount of money needed depends of course on the number of copies you want to print (calculated against expected sales, at a particular price). The more copies you order, the lower the unit-cost, but the more you will have to sell. Your pricing should allow for an important aspect of marketing: the giving away of review and complimentary copies. You also have to decide whether to budget for a profit (perhaps to use for the next publication) or just to break even. The overall cost can be reduced by supplying the printer with CRC on disk.

13. The great advantage of DTP, using a personal computer, is that it reduces costs. You can, if you want, be responsible for everything — including illustrations, the cover and binding. You can also print a relatively small number to test the market, and print more as needed. This method is ideal for relatively small publications of, say, fewer than thirty pages.

14. When individuals or groups publish for themselves, the final problem (and a big one) is marketing. It may be worth inviting selected guests and the media to a launch party; the cost in wine and nibbles can be offset by immediate sales of copies suitably signed or dedicated. If the launch can be made to coincide with an anniversary or a significant event such as a Local History Fair, so much the better. A new publication

---

[1] See *The Directory of Grant Making Trusts* (2 vols, 1997) which is regularly updated.

can be advertised by fliers and posters, and sold in a variety of outlets: shops, public institutions such as churches and libraries, and at local meetings and events. In approaching local newspapers, radio and TV, you are more likely to get mentioned if you go prepared with your own written summary of the project. Marketing success seems best assured when a group of people tout the publication on local doorsteps. The effort has to be continued until all the books are sold, or at least the outlay is recouped. Packages of unsold books are a nuisance and may be costly to store.

15. To get your publication noticed by other historians, make sure that copies are deposited in appropriate record offices, local-studies libraries and university libraries. Also send review copies to local newspapers, newsletters and journals, and to specialised national journals such as *The Local Historian*.[1] Finally, do not forget the legal obligation to deposit a copy at the Legal Deposit Office of the British Library, Boston Spa, Wetherby, West Yorkshire, LS23 7BY.[2]

---

[1] Where editors of journals are unable to review publications, they may merely list them. This is still a useful form of publicity.

[2] For a recent discussion of copyright and the six national copyright libraries, a subject which causes mystification and resentment, see Alan Crosby, 'Copyright Burdens on Local History', *Local History News* (BALH, No.48, Autumn 1998) p. 3.

11. FINAL REMINDERS

- If you feel tempted to write, give in,

- but take writing very seriously: it will outlive you.

- Do not keep postponing the start of writing.

- Make a preliminary plan and decide, roughly, how long a text you are aiming for. Be prepared to modify the plan as you write.

- Never cease reading the work of other historians, in and around your subject.

- Construct your writing around questions and problems, so that it reads as an logical argument or debate.

- Make sure that each paragraph is constructed around a single idea, and is not too long or too short.

- Control the length of your sentences. A short sentence can be very powerful.

- Do not let sources dominate your writing: you are in charge.

- Limit the use of quotations to those which are relevant and telling.

- Use as much detail as is necessary to sustain your argument, and no more.

- Do not necessarily expect to write the text from A to Z: parts can be written out of order and fitted together at a later stage.

- Revise your writing, as many times as it takes.

- Invite the criticism of others.

12. FURTHER READING

WRITING, GENERAL

Butcher, J., *Copy-editing: The Cambridge Handbook for Editors, Authors and Publishers* (CUP, 3rd edn, 1992)

Cutts, M., *The Plain English Guide* (OUP, 1995)

Fowler, H. W. & Fowler, F. G., *The King's English* (OUP, 3rd edn, 1996)

Gowers, E., *The Complete Plain Words* (Penguin, 3rd edn, 1987)

Hart's Rules for Compositors and Readers at the University Press, Oxford (39th edn, revised, 1983)

Maney, A. S. & Smallwood, R. L. (eds), *MHRA Style Book: Notes for Authors, Editors and Writers of Dissertations* (Modern Humanities Research Association, 1981)

Newby, M., *Writing: A Guide for Students* (1989)

Notes to OUP Authors (or notes provided by any other major publisher)

Orwell, G., 'Politics and the English Language' (written 1946), published in *Inside the Whale and Other Essays* (Penguin, 1962), 143-57

Robbins, R. M., 'Anniversary Address', *Antiquaries Jour.*, lxviii, pt 1 (1988), 3-8

St George, A. & F., *Clear English* (1996)

The Oxford Dictionary for Writers and Editors (Clarendon Press, 1981)

Writers' and Artists' Yearbook (annually, A. & C. Black)

LOCAL HISTORY

Bettey, J. H., *Church and Parish: An Introduction for Local Historians* (Batsford, 1987)

Bloomfield, B. C. (ed.), *A Directory of Rare Book and Special Collections in the United Kingdom and the Republic of Ireland* (2nd edn, 1997)

Bristow, J., *The Local Historian's Glossary and Vade Mecum* (Univ. of Nottingham, 2nd edn, 1994)

Cannadine, D. & Reeder, D. (eds), *Exploring the Urban Past: Essays in Urban History by H. J. Dyos* (CUP, 1982)

Caunce, S., *Oral History and the Local Historian* (Longman, 1994)

Colwell, S., *Dictionary of Genealogical Sources in the Public Record Office* (Weidenfeld & Nicolson, 1992)

Cox, M., *Exploring Scottish History: A Directory of Resource Centres for Scottish Local and National History in Scotland* (Scottish Library Assocn and Scottish Local History Forum, 1992).

Currie, C. R. J. & Lewis, C. P. (eds), *English County Histories: A Guide* (Alan Sutton, 1994)

Drake, M. & Finnegan, R. (eds), *Sources and Methods for Family and Community Historians: A Handbook* (CUP & Open Univ., 1994)

Edwards, P., *Rural Life: Guide to Local Records* (Batsford, 1993)

Elton, A., Harrison, B. & Wark, K., *Researching the Country House: A Guide for Local Historians* (Batsford, 1992)

Finberg, H. P. R., 'How Not to Write Local History' in Finberg, H. P. R. & Skipp, V. H. T., *Local History: Objective and Pursuit* (1967)

Finberg, H. P. R. & Skipp, V. H. T., *Local History: Objective and Pursuit* (David & Charles, 1967)

Foster, J. & Sheppard, J., *British Archives: A Guide to Archive Resources in the United Kingdom* (Macmillan, 3rd edn, 1995)

Glennie, P., *'Distinguishing Men's Trades': Occupational Sources and Debates for Pre-Census England* (Historical Geography Research Series, 25, 1990)

Guy, S., *English Local Studies Handbook: A Guide to Resources for each County, including Libraries, Record Offices, Societies, Journals and Museums* (Univ. of Exeter Press, 1992)

Hey, D., *Family History and Local History in England* (Longman, 1987)

Hey, D. (ed.), *The Oxford Companion to Local and Family History* (OUP, 1996)

Hoskins, W. G., *Local History in England* (Longman, 3rd edn, 1984)

Hoskins, W. G., *Fieldwork in Local History* (Faber, 2nd edn, 1982)

Kammen, C., *The Pursuit of Local History: Readings on Theory and Practice* (Altamira Press with American Assocn for State and Local History, 1996)

Lewis, C., *Particular Places: An Introduction to English Local History* (British Library, 1989)

Marshall, J. D., *The Tyranny of the Discrete: A Discussion of the Problems of Local History in England* (Scolar Press, 1997)

Moody, D., *Scottish Local History: An Introductory Guide* (Batsford, 1986)

Mullins, E. L. C., *Texts and Calendars: An Analytical Guide to Serial Publications* (Royal Hist. Soc., 2nd edn, 1983)

Munby, L. M. & Thompson, K. M. (eds), *Short Guides to Records* (Historical Assocn; 1st series, 1994; 2nd series, 1997)

Phythian-Adams, C., *Re-thinking English Local History* (Leicester UP, 1987)

Pinhorn, M., *Historical, Archaeological and Kindred Societies in Gt Britain: A Geographical List* (Pinhorns, 1995)

Porter, S., *Exploring Urban History: Sources for Local Historians* (Batsford, 1990)

Ravensdale, J. R., *History on your Doorstep* (BBC, 1982)

Raymond, S. A. (ed.), *British Genealogical Bibliographies* (Federation of Family History Societies; in progress by county)

Riden, P., *Local History: A Handbook for Beginners* (2nd edn, 1998)

Rogers, A., *Approaches to Local History* (Longman, 2nd edn, 1977)

Rogers, A. (ed.), *Group Projects in Local History* (Dawson, 1977)

Rogers, C. D. & Smith, J. H., *Local Family History in England* (Manchester UP, 1991)

Royal Comm. Hist. Manuscripts, *Record Repositories in Great Britain* (PRO Publications, 10th edn, 1997)

Royle, E. (ed.), *Issues of Regional Identity, In Honour of John Marshall* (Manchester Univ. Press, 1998)

Samuel, R., *Theatres of Memory, Vol 1: Past and Present in Contemporary Culture* (Verso, 1994)

Schurer, K. & Arkell, T., *Surveying the People* (Local Population Studies Supplement, 1992)

Sinclair, C., *Tracing Scottish Local History: A Guide to Local History Research in the Scottish Record Office* (HMSO, 1994)

Stapleton, B., 'Sources for the Demographic Study of a Local Community from the 16th to the mid-19th Century', *Journal of Regional & Local Studies*, vol.4, no.2 (1984), 1-26

Stephens, W. B., *Sources for English Local History* (CUP, 2nd edn, 1981)

Stevenson, D. & Stevenson, W., *Scottish Texts and Calendars: An Analytical Guide to Serial Publications* (Royal Hist. Soc. & Scottish History Soc., 1987)

Tate. W. E., *The Parish Chest: A Study of the Records of Parochial Administration in England* (3rd edn, Phillimore, 1983)

The Common Chronicle (V. & A. Museum, 1983)

Tiller, K., *English Local History: An Introduction* (Alan Sutton, 1992)

Tiller, K., *English Local History: The State of the Art* (Univ. of Cambridge Board of Continuing Education, Occasional Paper, No.1, 1998)

Williams, M. A., *Researching Local History: The Human Journey* (Longman, 1996)

Winge, H., 'Local History' in Hubbard, W. H. *et al.* (eds), *Making a Historical Culture: Historiography in Norway* (Scandinavian University Press, 1995)

Wrightson, K., 'The Politics of the Parish in Early Modern England' in Griffiths, P., Fox, A. & Hindle, S. (eds), *The Experience of Authority in Early Modern England* (1996)

Youngs, F. A., *Guide to the Local Administrative Units of England,Vol. 1: Southern England; Vol.II: Northern England*, Royal Hist. Soc., Guides & Handbooks, nos 10 (1979), 17 (1991).

SOME CLASSIC LOCAL STUDIES

Dyos, H. J., *Victorian Suburb: A Study of the Growth of Camberwell* (Leicester Univ. Press, 1961).

Goodacre, J., *The Transformation of a Peasant Economy: Townspeople and Villagers in the Lutterworth Area, 1500-1700* (1994).

Hey, D. G., *An English Rural Community: Myddle under the Tudors and Stuarts* (Leicester Univ. Press, 1974).

Hoskins, W. G., *The Midland Peasant: The Economic and Social History of a Leicestershire Village* [Wigston Magna], (Macmillan, 1965).

Levine, D. & Wrightson, K., *The Making of an Industrial Society: Whickham, 1560-1765* (Oxford, 1991).

McIntosh, M. K., *Autonomy and Community: The Royal Manor of Havering, 1200-1500* (1986)

McIntosh, M. K., *A Community Transformed: The Manor and Liberty of Havering, 1500-1620* (1991)

Marcombe, D., *English Small Town Life: Retford, 1520-1642* (Univ. of Nottingham, 1993).

Nair, G., *Highley: The Development of a Community, 1550-1880* (Basil Blackwell, 1988).

Prior, M., *Fisher Row: Fishermen, Bargemen and Canal Boatmen in Oxford, 1500-1900* (1982)

Shaw, D. G., *The Creation of a Community: The City of Wells in the Middle Ages* (Oxford, 1993).

Skipp, V., *Crisis and Development: An Ecological Case Study of the Forest of Arden, 1570-1674* (CUP, 1978).

Spufford, M., *Contrasting Communities: English Villagers in the Sixteenth and Seventeenth Centuries* (CUP, 1974).

Summerson, H. R. T., *Medieval Carlisle: The City and the Borders from the Late 11th to the Mid-16th Century* (2 vols, 1993).

Underdown, D., *Fire from Heaven: Life in an English Town in the Seventeenth Century* [Dorchester], (Harper Collins, 1992).

Wrightson, K. & Levine, D., *Poverty and Piety in an English Village: Terling, 1525-1700* (2nd edn, Oxford, 1995)

JOURNALS OF LOCAL AND REGIONAL HISTORY

The Local Historian (published quarterly by The British Association for Local History)

The Local History Magazine (published six times a year by The Local History Press, Nottingham)

Journal of Regional and Local Studies (published twice yearly by the Univ. of Lincolnshire and Humberside, with assistance from The Conference of Regional and Local Historians)

Local Population Studies (published twice yearly by The Cambridge Group for the History of Population and Social Structure)

Family and Community History (published twice a year for the Family and Community Historical Research Society)

Northern History (published annually from School of History, Univ. of Leeds)
Midland History (published annually by Univ. of Birmingham)
Southern History (published annually by Southern History Society)
The Scottish Historical Review (published twice yearly by Edinburgh Univ. Press)
Northern Scotland (published annually by the Centre for Scottish Studies, Univ. of Aberdeen)
The Welsh History Review (published twice yearly by Univ. of Wales Press)

HISTORICAL METHODS

Barzun, J. & Graff, H. F., *The Modern Researcher* (Fort Worth, 5th edn, *c.*1992)

Cheney, C. R. (ed.), *Handbook of Dates for Students of English History* (CUP, 1995)

Forde, H. & Seton, R. (eds), *Archivists and Researchers: Mutual Perceptions and Requirements* (BRA, 1994)

Fryde, E. B., Greenway, D. E., Porter, S. & Roy, I., *Handbook of British Chronology* (Royal Hist. Soc., Guides & Handbooks, no.2; CUP, 3rd edn, 1996)

Greenstein, D. I., *A Historian's Guide to Computing* (OUP, 1994)

Hunnisett, R. F., *Editing Records for Publication* (BRA, Archives & the User, no.4, 1977)

Hunnisett. R. F., *Indexing for Editors* (BRA, Archives & the User, no.2, 1972)

Kitching, C., *Archives: The very Essence of our Heritage* (Phillimore, 1996)

Lewis, M. J. & Lloyd-Jones, R., *Using Computers in History: A Practical Guide* (Routledge, 1996)

Macfarlane, A., *Reconstructing Historical Communities* (CUP, 1977)

Mawdsley, E. & Munck, T., *Computing for Historians: An Introductory Guide* (Manchester UP, 1993)

Olney, R. J., *Manuscript Sources for British History: Their Nature, Location and Use* (Inst. Historical Research Guides, 3, 1995)

Perks, R., *Oral History: Talking about the Past* (Historical Assoc., 2nd edn, 1995)

Tosh, J., *The Pursuit of History: Aims, Methods and New Directions in the Study of Modern History* (Longman, 2nd edn, 1991)

Trubshaw, R. N., *How to Write and Publish Local History* (Heart of Albion Press, 1999)

APPENDICES

Appendix 1

PUBLISHED RESOURCES

The purpose of this appendix is to stress the importance of printed materials which local historians can never afford to ignore. Mainly to be found in major or specialist libraries, they include 'primary sources' which have been transcribed, translated and calendared (summarised); various guides, lists and indexes which point to original manuscripts; and the written interpretative work of historians which form 'secondary sources'.

A. Transcripts, Translations and Calendars of Primary Sources

- Over more than two centuries, a vast amount of original evidence referring to local communities has appeared in print in the form of transcriptions and translations. For a general introduction to these, see E. L. C. Mullins, *Texts and Calendars* (1983). This book lists the publications of the Record Commissioners who were set up in 1800, of the Public Record Office, of national record societies (e.g. Camden, Selden and Harleian), and of more local record societies (e.g. Surtees, Norfolk and Bristol).[1]

- In the early 19th century, the Record Commissioners published transcripts of many important documents with wide geographical coverage (e.g. the Hundred Rolls of the late 13th century, the Ecclesiastical Taxation of 1291, the Inquisition of the Ninth of 1340/1, and the *Valor Ecclesiasticus* of 1535).

- A local historian should always be prepared to search through official calendars (e.g. the Patent Rolls, Close Rolls, Charter Rolls, Inquisitions Post Mortem, Acts of the Privy Council, and Letters and Papers of the Reign of Henry VIII). Such volumes are usually indexed, though not always adequately by modern standards. A small book called *British National Archives, Sectional List No. 24* lists all the officially published indexes, transcripts and calendars of documents in the national archives. While working through such volumes in a library, it is useful to be able to tick them off on this list.

---

[1] The Historical Manuscripts Commission now updates this list on the world-wide web. The address is: http://www.hmc.gov.uk

- Another great series of calendars has been produced by the Historical Manuscripts Commission (HMC), listing and abstracting major collections belonging to individuals, estates, corporations, dioceses, etc.
- Considerable riches lie in a series called *Records of Early English Drama* (*REED*), published by the University of Toronto Press since 1979. The aim is 'to find, transcribe and publish external evidence of dramatic, ceremonial and minstrel activity in Gt Britain before 1642'. Volumes deal with individual counties and cities.
- Local historians working in the north of England should scan the series known as *Borthwick Texts and Calendars: Records of the Northern Province* (published by the University of York).
- It should not be forgotten that individual historians and antiquaries have published and edited texts, sometimes singly and sometimes in series (e.g. transcripts of parish registers, collections of wills, etc.)
- An astonishing amount of material has appeared for generations in the form of Notes & Queries and Miscellanies (e.g. *Devon & Cornwall Notes & Queries* from 1901, and *East Anglian Miscellany*, also from 1901).
- County historical and archaeological journals contain many transcripts and translations of original documents, usually embedded in articles.
- The text of Domesday Book can be found in the general volumes published for each county by the *VCH*, and in a new indexed series published by Phillimore.

B. Indexes and Guides to Primary Sources

- The *Guide to the Public Records*, 2 vols (1963) gives general guidance on the contents of the Public Record Office at Kew (PRO). For example it will tell you that lists of church goods taken in the reigns of Edward VI and Mary are to be found under E117, and that the Corn Returns of 1799 to 1949 are under MAF10. Another good general introduction to the PRO is Philip Riden's *Local History: A Handbook for Beginners* (revised 1998).
- More detailed are the *PRO Lists and Indexes* and the parallel productions of the List and Index Society. These give references to individual documents with brief details of contents, places and personal names. The scores of volumes already printed cover, for example, many manorial documents kept in the PRO (court rolls, ministers' accounts and surveys), proceedings of the Star Chamber, registers of the Society of Friends, tithe files, and acreage returns of 1801.
- Some county record offices publish guides to their own sources. Newsletters, lists of accessions and hand-outs are also produced to help searchers.
- Early printed 'books', from the 15th century to the 19th, are listed in *Short Title Catalogues* [STC]: 3 vols for the period 1475-1640; 3 vols for 1641-1700; 5 vols for

the 18th century; 6 vols for 1801-15; 56 vols for 1816-70. This is major resource which local historians often neglect.

• A vast amount of original evidence for local communities lies buried in *British Parliamentary Papers* [BPP]. Useful guidance can be found in W. R. Powell, *Local History from Blue Books* (1962), but the fullest and most up-to-date introduction is P. Cockton, *Subject Catalogue of the House of Commons Parliamentary Papers, 1801-1900* (5 vols, Chadwyck-Healey, 1988).

• Many guides are available for specific types of document. Good examples are M. W. Barley, *A Guide to British Topographical Collections* (CBA, 1974), *Newsplan* (volumes surveying local newspapers; published by the British Library) and R. W. Cox, *Index to Sporting Manuscripts in the UK* (British Soc. of Sports History, 1995). No local historian should neglect the numerous guides produced for family historians, and often published by the Federation of Family History Societies. Recent examples from the pen of Jeremy Gibson, and frequently updated, include *Poll Books, c.1696-1872* (3rd edn, 1994), *Quarter Sessions Records for Family Historians* (4th edn, 1995) and *Coroners' Records in England & Wales* (2nd edn, 1997).

• The Royal Commission on Historical Manuscripts (Quality House, Quality Court, Chancery Lane, London WC2A 1HP) has two resources of great value: the National Register of Archives which contains thousands of unpublished lists and catalogues of manuscript collections, and the Manorial Documents Register.

C. Secondary Sources

• The local historian's principal route to secondary sources (that is, the published work of other historians) must be through references, bibliographies, reviews and abstracts (see pp. 36-8, above).

• Regional and county bibliographies listing all kinds of published history are particularly valuable, where they exist. See for example *A Bibliography of Norfolk History*, edited by E. Darroch and B. Taylor (1975).

• Of all printed sources, the most obvious for the local historian are the large red tomes of the *VCH*. Though this project to provide a detailed history for every English county is incomplete, over 200 volumes are currently available. They are of two kinds. 'General volumes' have valuable chapters on subjects such as religious history and agriculture, while 'topographical volumes' contain the histories of individual parishes and towns. Local historians working in counties *without* topographical coverage will still learn a lot from the *VCH* of other counties — about basic sources and about the infinite variety of human communities. Work on this scholarly enterprise still continues in about a dozen counties.

• Another detailed survey can be found in inventories of the three Royal Commissions on Historical / Ancient Monuments, recording the buildings, monuments and archaeological sites of England, Wales and Scotland. Coverage, however, is still incomplete.

- For basic architectural comment, at parish level, see the indispensable Penguin series, *The Buildings of England/Scotland/Wales/Ireland*, still known affectionately as 'Pevsner'.

- For archaeological background the local historian should scan titles in two long series: *Research Reports* of the Council for British Archaeology (CBA), and *British Archaeological Reports, British Series* (*BAR*).

- Obvious sources of comparative information include parish, town and county histories, of any date; the journals of local historical and archaeological societies; and the more ephemeral bulletins and newsletters also published by local societies and research groups. It hardly needs saying that the local historian should not search merely for the name of his or her own 'place', but should be prepared to learn from wider trawling (see pp. 24-5).

- Of great value is the *Annual Bulletin of Historical Literature: A Critical Review of New Publications*, published by the Historical Association. This provides 'a selective and critical review of recent historical books, journals and articles covering all periods of history'. Sections deal primarily with periods (e.g. 'Later Middle Ages' and 'Nineteenth Century') and are sub-divided by subjects (e.g. 'Political and Religious History' and 'Economic and Social History'), and by national areas (e.g. England, Scotland, Wales and Ireland). This review makes frequent reference to localised work, including examples published in regional journals, record series and occasionally in county journals.

- Bibliographies of a more thematic kind are also worth searching. For example: A. T. Hall, *English Local History Handlist*, *A Select Bibliography and Guide to Sources* (HA, Helps to Students of History, 69, 5th edn, nd. [up to 1979]); Owen Chadwick, *The History of the Church, A Select Bibliography*; and *A Bibliography of Vernacular Architecture* (four edns, 1972, 1979, 1992 and 1999). It is sad that the numerous bibliographies which academics prepare for their own students are not collected and published for wider consumption. This is a service which could now be done, and regularly updated, on the Internet.

- Because local history has imprecise boundaries, we must keep an eye on new books and the latest issues of journals in several other historical specialisations. Obviously relevant journals include *History*, *Landscape History*, *Local Population Studies*, *Economic History Review*, *Agricultural History Review*, *Rural History*, *Urban History* and the *Journal of Ecclesiastical History*.

Appendix 2

RECORDING THE PRESENT

The best-known examples of this historical approach in Great Britain are undoubtedly the three *Statistical Accounts of Scotland*, which were published in 1791-9 (21 volumes), 1845 (15 volumes) and 1951-92 (28 volumes). Opposite is a sample drawn from the last volume of the *Third Account*, part of Thomas Hedley's description of the parish of Ancrum, Roxburghshire, written in 1984 and published in 1992. Inevitably it contains personal judgements and even prejudices, but that does not invalidate the value of such writing for the future. Here a local resident takes on the role of contemporary historian, akin to that of the medieval chronicler, ensuring that the trends of late-20th century life are described by one who has actually experienced them. All local communities deserve to have such records, preferably updated at regular intervals.

Garage and Petrol Pumps — Both are now closed, the nearest of these services now being at Bonjedward.

Police Station — There is no longer a resident policeman and the old police-house is now privately owned and occupied. Police services are all centralised in Hawick. There appears, however, to be adequate police supervision in the village.

Postal Services — For Ancrum, as for many other rural areas, collection and delivery of mail are now centralised through the bigger town Post Offices. Ancrum no longer has its own village postman, delivering at least twice daily — and being ever ready to do local errands for villagers in addition! There is now one daily delivery through the Jedburgh office, with thrice daily collections of mail. With the village sub-Post Office still functioning, the parish is still reasonably well served; but much still depends on its continued existence.

The Smithy — This was re-opened and flourished for a time during the 1960s. It was then closed and sold as a private dwelling; and today all that reminds one of its having existed is the name 'Smithy House'.

Tradesmen's Vans — The daily visits of bakery, greengrocery and butcher vans are very much a thing of the past. There are still some vanmen who call weekly; but much of their business is now carried on by the two general stores. Ancrum is fortunate, however, in having the services of at least five coal-merchants providing weekly or fortnightly visits.

Joinery — Only one joiner's business remains, but the premises of the one who retired have now been taken over by a local plumber, thus providing a **new** local service.

From the early 1960s shopping outside the village was made somewhat difficult by the structure of bus-timetabling offered to those dependent on such services. Bus trips to town (Jedburgh) offered two possibilities — either a very hurried visit in order to catch the return bus, or the prospect of having to spend far longer than necessary to obtain one's requirements. More recently there has been some improvement, but in rural areas private cars are now more a matter of necessity than of luxury.

Allowing for all the changes, Ancrum is well served by its local shops and tradesmen. If desired, all foodstuffs and household requirements are available at the two shops and the services of a joiner, a plumber and a painter/decorator are at hand.

Ancrum still has one inn, the Cross Keys, presently under new owners and undergoing some alterations. One welcome addition to

Third Statistical Account of Scotland: Extract, 1992

Appendix 3

TRANSCRIBING DOCUMENTS: BASIC RULES

1. The aim is to reproduce the text as accurately as possible: nothing is to be added or omitted without acknowledgement in a key or footnote.
2. Any editorial insertions made by the transcriber should be italicised (or underlined) within square brackets. For example: [*illegible*] or [*change of handwriting*].
3. Each transcript should be headed with a reference to both repository and document. For example: PRO, E179/260/5.
4. The numbers of pages, folios or membranes should be shown at the appropriate points in the text. For front and back faces of each folio, use 'r' (*recto*) and 'v' (*verso*); for the back of a membrane use 'd' (*dorso*).
5. An oblique stroke can be used to show where each line of the original document ends, thus /. In the case of a complicated manuscript with sub-headings and marginal notes, however, it is probably best to replicate the original layout.
6. Retain the original spelling, however idiosyncratic or inconsistent. Also retain the original punctuation (if it exists), marginal headings, paragraphing and capital letters (however odd their distribution). Do not at this stage add your own punctuation or 'correct' the spelling.
7. However, the Anglo-Saxon 'thorn' (þ) should be transcribed as 'th', which is what was intended, and not as 'y'. Thus 'the chirche', not 'ye chirche'.[1] Similarly, it is much better to use 'u', 'v' and 'n' as pronounced, and not as written. Thus, 'havyng' rather than 'hauyng'.
8. Numbers should be given as in the original (whether Roman, Arabic or a mixture of the two).
9. Insertions should be distinguished (see conventions below).
10. Deletions should be noted, and transcribed if legible (see conventions below).
11. Abbreviations which are readily understood should be extended and acknowledged (see conventions below).

---

[1] However, the Anglo-Saxon 'yogh' (ȝ) should be noted as such, because it represents a sound (a soft 'g') which cannot be translated exactly into modern orthography. For example, 'ȝevyn' which stands for the modern 'given'.

12. If you have any doubts about the reading of a word or number, insert an italic question-mark immediately in front of it (without a space) and within square brackets, thus [*?*].

13. To show that an error is in the manuscript itself, and is not the fault of the transcriber, use [*sic*] meaning 'thus'.

14. Always re-check your transcript against the original. And check it again before publication.

CONVENTIONS RECOMMENDED FOR TRANSCRIBING

For insertions	\ /
For deletions	< >
For items illegible or damaged	[…] or [*illeg.*], [*damaged*] or <*illeg.*> if deleted
For unfilled spaces in text	[*blank*]
For doubtful readings	[?] immediately preceding word or number in question, without a space.
For abbreviations	Underline restored letters, thus 'pa<u>ri</u>sh<u>i</u>oners', or put them in square brackets, thus 'app[ur]tena[u]nc[es]'. If you are uncertain, e.g. about a Latin case-ending, it is safer to put an apostrophe for the part omitted, thus *messuag'*.

PUBLISHING TRANSCRIPTS

When a transcript is published, it is legitimate to help readers by making certain changes to the text. For example, one can extend obvious abbreviations without acknowledgement, convert Roman to Arabic figures, modernise the use of capital and lower-case letters, and introduce modern punctuation providing no contentious meaning is imposed. One should explain the conventions used, and any other *ad hoc* decisions, in an introductory note or key. For an example of such changes, see below (p. 99-102).

EXAMPLES OF TRANSCRIPTION

1. Letter from Eleanor, Countess of Cumberland, to her husband Henry, 2nd Earl of Cumberland, undated but *c.*1547: Cumbria Record Office (Kendal), WD/Hoth/ box 44 (with grateful acknowledgement to Lord Hothfield and the Cumbria Record Office)

Transcription

Jh<u>es</u>us

1   dere hart af<u>ter</u> my moste hartye Comendatyons/ thys shalbe
2   to s<u>er</u>tefy yow th<u>at</u> sens yo<u>ur</u> departure frome me I have bene
3   very seke & att thys p<u>re</u>sent my watt<u>er</u> ys very Redd where
4   by I suppos I have the Jaun<u>ne</u>s & the aygew bothe for I
5   have none abytyde to meat' & I have suche payns in my
6   syde & toward<u>es</u> <..> my bak' as I had att browham when
7   ytt be gane w<u>i</u>th me furst where for I desyre yow to
8   help me to a physyssyon & th<u>at</u> thys berar may brynge
9   hym w<u>i</u>th hym/ for now in the begynnyng I trust
10   I may have gud remedy & the longer ytt ys drevyn'
11   the worse ytt wylbe/ also my syst<u>er</u> powys ys <..>com<u>m</u>yd
12   to me & ys very desyrous to se yow whych<u>e</u> I trust
13   shalbe the so<u>u</u>ner at thys tyme & thus Jh<u>es</u>u send hus
14   bothe healthe/ att my lodg' of Carleton the xiiijth
15   day of februarij
16   gud dere hart' I pray yow send for doctor stephyns
17   for he knawythe best my complexon for suche cawsys

18   by your assuryd loufeng'
19   wyff Elenor Cu<u>m</u>barland

Notes

The original layout of lines has been retained (each numbered for ease of reference). Capital letters, dashes for occasional punctuation and the ampersand (&) are given as in the original. Where no uncertainty exists, the spelling of abbreviated words has been extended, but the restored letters are underlined. A flourish at the end of some words has been rendered by an apostrophe; some palaeographers would append a final 'e'.

line 4: the word 'jaundice' is spelt with four minims and has an abbreviation sign over it, so a 'u' has been introduced.

lines 6 and 11: small and illegible deletions are shown by angle brackets and dots.

line 19: the final signature is in a different hand.

The above is an attempt at a completely accurate transcript. In a published version (whether in a record volume or simply in a quotation), one can justifiably introduce certain, relatively light, changes as an aid to the reader (see above, p. 97). The above letter might appear in print as follows:

Dere hart. After my moste hartye comendatyons, thys shalbe to sertefy yow that sens your departure frome me I have bene very seke and att thys present my watter ys very redd, where by I suppos I have the jaunnes and the aygew bothe, for I have none abytyde to meat', and I have suche payns in my syde and towardes <..> my bak' as I had att Browham when ytt be gane with me furst. Where for I desyre yow to help me to a physyssyon, and that thys berar may brynge hym with hym. For now in the begynnyng I trust I may have gud remedy, and the longer ytt ys drevyn the worse ytt wylbe. Also my syster Powys ys <..>commyd to me and ys very desyrous to se yow, whyche I trust shalbe the souner at thys tyme, and thus Jhesu send hus bothe healthe. Att my lodg' of Carleton, the 14th day of Februarii.

 Gud dere hart', I pray yow send for Doctor Stephyns, for he knawythe best my complexon for suche cawsys. By your assuryd loufeng' wyff, Elenor Cumbarland.

2. Churchwardens' Account, Ely Holy Trinity, 1577: Cambridgeshire Record Office, P67/5/1 [*facsimile opposite*]

Transcription

The accomptantes praye to be allowed — xvj^{d.} payd
for the foure quarter dayes to the parator &
— viij^{d.} for ij keyes mendinge — xvj^{d.} for
washinge the churche clothes & v^{li'} delivered unto
Thomas Darnell thelder & Edmund Slowe
toward the howse of correction & — xx^{s.} delivered toe
Tyllingham with a poore wenche of Turpins and

Allowances — x^{s.} vij^{d.} ob' spent at divers times about the   vij^{li'} iij^{s.} iij^{d.} ob'
Communion & — xvj^{d.} payd for the gatheringe
of the monye for the communion & — iij^{s.} iiij^{d.}
payd to the distributers for vermen & — xij^{d.}
payd for a case for the communion Cup & — xij^{d.}
for a coppye of a writt and — xij^{d.} spent at
the takinge of the last accompt & — xx^{d.} for
drawinge and entringe this accompt.

Summa allocacionis — vij^{li'} iij^{s.} iij^{d.} ob'

Notes

The original layout of lines and marginal entries has been retained; where words were abbreviated, restored letters are underlined. However, to reflect normal usage over the centuries, the abbreviations for pounds, shillings and pence are retained, but superscript; similarly ob' (Latin *obulus* = halfpenny) is left unextended. The horizontal line and decorative 'pip' before most sums of money has been rendered simply by a dash.

In published form, accounts usually need to be laid out quite generously, with careful punctuation and indentations, so that different items appear on separate lines. (To put them into continuous blocks of prose makes reading much more difficult.) It also helps to convert Roman to Arabic numerals. The above account might be printed or quoted as follows:

Allowances [*in margin*]
    The accomptantes praye to be allowed:
    16d. payd for the foure quarter dayes to the parator,
    and 8d. for two keyes mendinge,
    and 16d. for washinge the churche clothes,
    and £5 delivered unto Thomas Darnell thelder and Edmund Slowe
        toward the howse of correction,
    and 20s. delivered toe Tyllingham with a poore wenche of Turpins,

and 10s. 7½d. spent at divers times about the communion,

and 16d. payd for the gatheringe of the monye for the communion,

and 3s. 4d. payd to the distributers for vermen,

and 12d. payd for a case for the communion cup,

and 12d. for a coppye of a writt,

and 12d. spent at the takinge of the last accompt,

and 20d. for drawinge and entringe this accompt.

Summa allocacionis, £7 3s. 3½d.

If the editing were stronger still, one might drop the repetitive 'ands', and put the sums of money in tabulated form on the right-hand side of the text (such changes would have to be scrupulously acknowledged in footnotes or special Editorial Notes). For example:

	[£	s.	d.]
Allowances [*in margin*]			
The accomptantes praye to be allowed:			
payd for the foure quarter dayes to the parator			16
for two keyes mendinge			8
for washinge the churche clothes			16
delivered unto Thomas Darnell thelder and Edmund			
Slowe toward the howse of correction	5	0	0
delivered toe Tyllingham with a poore wench			
of Turpins	1	0	0
spent at divers times about the communion		10	7½
[*etc., etc.*]			

Appendix 4

MAKING AN ABSTRACT: EXAMPLE

Abstracting is a way of 'gutting' an historical document, and recording it in a compact and modernised form. In a 'full abstract' every significant statement is carefully retained, but without transcribing every word or keeping to the original spelling. Many historians handle their documents in this way, and record societies frequently publish full abstracts because they save space and are more readily usable.[1] This important historical technique is illustrated below: a late-medieval will is given first as a verbatim transcript and then as a full abstract.

1. VERBATIM TRANSCRIPT

Will of John Smyth, chaplain of York, 10 August 1529
In dei nomine, Amen. The xth day of August in the yere of our Lord God Mv^Cxxix. I, John Smyth, preist in Sanct William chappell of Ouse briege in the citie of York of hooll mynde and good memorie dooith ordane and maik my testament and last will in this forme folowing. Furst I gyve and bequeith my saull to Almyghtie God, to our blissed Ladie Sanct Marie and to all the celestiall cowrt of heven, and my bodie to be buried in the church erth of Sanct John Appostle and Evangelist at thend of Ouse breige aforeseid. Item I bequeith to the church warkes their xxd. Item I bequeith to my broder Steven Smyth xiid. Item to Margaret my suster xiid. Item to my cosyne Christofer Magham viiid. Item to my kynswoman Malde Mawgham viiid. Item I bequeith to Sir John Stapleton a jaket of chamelet. Item I bequeith to Sir Henry Cookeson a dublet of chamelet with sarsenyt slevis. Item I will that all my brether in the said chappell of Ousebriege be at my derige and beriall and also all the preistes of Sanct John church aforeseid. The reist of my goodes not bequeithide, my dettes paid and my funerall expenses done, I gyve to William Smyth my brother, whome I make executor of this my present will and testament. And my cosyne Sir Adame, vicar of Acome, the seid Sir Henrie Cookson and Sir John Stapleton to be supervisoures hereof. Item I will that my

---

[1] For example, S. Lang & M. McGregor (eds), *Tudor Wills Proved in Bristol, 1546-1603*, Bristol Record Soc., xliv (1993); V. Harding & L. Wright (eds), *London Bridge: Selected Accounts and Rentals, 1381-1538* (London Record Soc., 1995).

brother Steven have the iii oxgange lande and the litle howse which was geven by the arbitrous. And I bequeith to the seid Sir Adame a silver spone. Theis witnes Sir Henrie Cookeson and Sir John Stapleton, preistes, with other.

Prob. 9 November 1529   (York Minster Library, D & C Prob. Reg. 2, fol.154r)

[From Claire Cross, *York Clergy Wills, 1520-1600: II City Clergy*, Borthwick Texts & Calendars 15, 1989, p. 10.]

2. FULL ABSTRACT

of the same will, in 167 words instead of 289. Notice that some words and phrases of special interest, or of uncertain significance, are given in their original spellings and in inverted commas. These could be used later as direct quotations in writing. Place-names and forenames are modernised, unless they are in some way doubtful, but for safety's sake surnames are left in their original spellings (with inconsistencies such as 'Cookeson' and 'Cookson').

Will of JOHN SMYTH, priest of St William's chapel on Ouse Bridge, York, 10 August 1529

Soul to Almighty God, St Mary and 'all the celestiall cowrt of heven'.

To be buried in St John's church at the end of Ouse Bridge ('in the church erth').

To repair ('church warkes') of St John's 20d.

To my brother Steven Smyth 12d.

To my sister Margaret 12d.

To my cousin Christopher Magham 8d.

To my kinswoman Maud Mawgham 8d.

To Sir John Stapleton a jacket of camlet ('chamelet').

To Sir Henry Cookeson a doublet of camlet with sarsenet ('sarsenyt') sleeves.

All my brethren in St William's chapel, and all the priests of St John's church, to attend my dirge and burial.

Residue, after payment of my debts and funeral expenses, to my brother William Smyth: executor.

Supervisors: my cousin Sir Adam, vicar of Acomb, Sir Henry Cookson and Sir John Stapleton.

To my brother Steven three oxgangs of land and 'the litle howse', given by the arbiters ('arbitrous').

To Sir Adam a silver spoon.

Witnesses: Sir Henry Cookeson and Sir John Stapleton, priests, and others.

Proved 9 November 1529.

(York Minster Library, D & C Prob. Reg. 2, fol.154r)

Appendix 5

HISTORICAL DATING: WITH EXERCISES

To convert a medieval date to modern style, the following procedure should be followed. Using C. R. Cheney's *Handbook of Dates for Students of English History* (latest edition, CUP, 1995):

1. Identify the date of the feast (pp. 43-64).
2. Convert the regnal year into one or two calendar years (pp. 13-31). In the vast majority of cases, the regnal year straddles two calendar years (each of which has a reference number to the right).
3. If, as is usually the case, your date does not fall exactly on the feast day but on 'the Thursday before' or 'the Monday after', note the number given opposite the relevant calendar year on pp. 13-31. This is turn refers you to a table somewhere between pp. 84 and 155.
4. Turn to the relevant table, and identify the precise day of the month.

WARNING: if the day falls in January or February, be careful to note whether you are, or are not, in a leap year (in its heading each table identifies leap years in bold print). If yours is indeed a leap year, use the two columns for Jan. and Feb. which are on the extreme left of the table.

EXERCISES

Using the methods described above, convert the following into modern-style dates (day of the month and/or year):

1. Feast of St Bartholomew the Apostle
2. Feast of St Zita of Lucca
3. Feast of the Eleven Thousand Virgins (*Undecim millia virgines*)
4. Feast of the Second Translation of Edward King and Martyr
5. Feast of *Corpus Christi*
6. 4 Edward I
7. 21 Richard II
8. 38 Henry VIII
9. 12 Charles II

10. Saturday after the Feast of St Ambrose, 2 Edward II
11. Friday before the Nativity of the Blessed Virgin Mary, 10 Edward III
12. Saturday after the Feast of St Luke the Evangelist, 21 Richard II
13. Wednesday before the Decollation of St John the Baptist, 38 Henry VI
14. Thursday before Candlemas, 50 Edward III
15. 9th January, 1704/5

(Answers are given on p.160)

Appendix 6

ANALYSIS OF DOCUMENTS — 1

The first example of analysis is based on a tax list. Many sources available to local historians are of this simple form: lists of names, sums of money and other details for individual parishes. At first sight they may appear of only limited historical and genealogical value, but in fact they can be systematically analysed to reveal important social and economic differences within and between parishes.

The Hearth Tax assessments of 1665 for three adjacent rural parishes in north Hampshire are reproduced overleaf from a local record series. They list personal names with the number of hearths on which each individual was assessed. Very few other details are given, apart from the occasional indication of social status or occupation.

ASSESSMENTS FOR HEARTH TAX

Transcripts sampled from E. Hughes & P. White (eds), *The Hampshire Hearth Tax Assessment, 1665,* **(Hampshire Record Series, 11, 1991), 248-9, 253-5**

The most obvious reaction to such a document (see overleaf) is to devise questions which will squeeze out more meaning, such as:

1. Number of taxpayers in the parish of *x*?
2. Number of people exempted from tax on grounds of poverty?
3. Proportion of those exempted?
4. Estimated total population? (A multiplier of 4.5 is often used.)[1]
5. Tabulate the distribution of hearths, to give some indication of social structure. (See example below, p. 109.)
6. Number of people with social status indicated? Give details.
7. Are occupations specified? If in sufficient numbers, count and classify them.
8. How many women? How many widows?
9. Are any 'addresses' given? Can they be identified on the ground?

---

[1] T. Arkell, 'Multiplying Factors for Estimating Population Totals from the Hearth Tax', *LPS*, 28 (1982).

FYFIELD		
Hearths chargeable		
Mister Lawrence	5	
Mister Winckworth	6	
William Blake	3	
Christopher Fleetwood	2	
John Kent	1	
Thomas Smith	1	
Mistress Wattson	1	
William Kenton	1	
Richard Hutchins	1	
John Clerke	1	
William Bedord	1	
John Mundy	2	
Peter Guye	1	
John Nuttkin	1	
William Collins	1	
Richard Bullock	3	
Matthew Gale	1	
Adam Holloway	1	
Thomas Clerke	1	
	hearths	34
Hearths not chargeable		
John Smith	1	
William Fuller	1	
Widow Beale	1	
Widow Hedd	1	
	hearths	4

THRUXTON		
Hearths chargeable		
Henry Rogers esquire	15	
John Fulker	5	
Michael Clerke	2	
James Easton	3	
George Downes	1	
Richard Carpenter	1	
Robert Berrett	1	
Richard Hyde	1	
Roger Hall	6	
Edward Miles	1	
William Ball	1	
Nicholas Bath	1	
John Woodward	1	
John Cowdrey	1	
John Downes	2	
Margaret Downes	1	
Barbara Franckline	1	
John Cuttler	1	
Mister William		
Chandler	1	
William Beale	3	
John Beale	2	
Thomas Beale	2	
Thomas Joyat	1	
Thomas Stockley senior	1	
Thomas Stockley junior	1	
	hearths	56
Hearths not chargeable		
John Downton	1	
Ursula Phillipps	1	
Robert Clerke	1	
William Cowdrey	1	
Hugh Collins	1	
Ellen Cowdrey	1	
Francis Harding	1	
Alice Goodale	1	
	hearths	8

APPLESHAW		
Hearths chargeable		
George Rumbold junior	2	
Thomas Meare	1	
John Gale senior	2	
John Ivye	2	
George Faye	2	
George Rumbold	1	
William Rumbold	2	
Nicholas Skeate	3	
Lancelot Browne	1	
Edmund Morrell	1	
Edward Browne	1	
Edward Blackmore	1	
William Ward	1	
Widow Isron	1	
Richard Crowch	1	
James Hellier	1	
	hearths	23
Hearths not chargeable		
Thomas Powell senior	1	
Thomas Powell junior	1	
Widow Allen	1	
William Warde	1	
William Washbeard	1	
John Skeate	1	
Richard Crowch	2	
Thomas Goyat	2	
Widow Goyat	1	
John Hunt	1	
Edward Addams	1	
Widow Crowch	1	
William Elton	1	
William Jowles	1	
Thomas Rumsey	1	
John Annett	1	
Widow Cole	1	
Ludd Biggs	1	
Robert Stulby	1	
Thomas Pewsey	1	
William Morrell	1	
Richard Morrell	1	
Edward Addams	1	
William Gasthall	1	
John Crowch	1	
Jasper Smith	1	
Thomas Dummer	1	
Richard Dummer	1	
Edward Williams	1	
Philip Allen	1	
Elizabeth Heyter	1	
Edward Addams junior	1	
John Hyde	1	
Widow Crowch	2	
	hearths	37

Hearth Tax Returns for Three Hampshire Parishes, 1665: Published Transcript

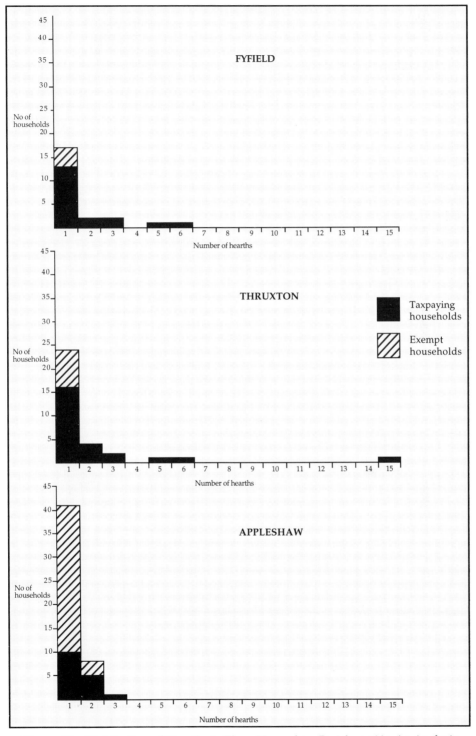

Fig. 3   The Distribution of Hearths in Three Hampshire Parishes 1665: An Analysis

10. Is the list arranged socially, topographically, or by a mixture of the two? (Some tax-lists reveal the route taken by assessors and collectors.)

11. Are any extra comments given, as in the Cornish returns?[1]

After analysing the data for a single parish, one can profitably extend the work to surrounding parishes, or to a much wider district. Invariably this reveals instructive and sometimes surprising differences. Local surnames can be compared with those given in other tax lists, in the same or different periods. In Norfolk for example, McKinley found that only 20 per cent of the surnames listed in the Lay Subsidy of 1524 were still in the same parishes when the Hearth Tax was assessed in 1666. Fig.3, on the previous page, tabulates the distribution of hearths in the three Hampshire parishes listed above, on the assumption that the number of hearths in each household reflects wealth and social status.

Clearly these three parishes in 1665 varied in overall size and in social composition. Fyfield, the smallest, had three resident gentry and five middling householders with three to six hearths. The rest of the population, including a poor gentlewoman, had single hearths, yet interestingly only four of them were considered too poor to pay the tax. Thruxton was rather larger, again with a middling element of five households but dominated by one wealthy gentleman living in a large house with fifteen hearths.[2] At the bottom end of the social scale were four families with two hearths and twenty-four with one. Of those with one hearth, one-third were officially classed as poor. Appleshaw, the third and largest community, had a much more even social structure and was obviously poorer than its neighbours. Only one householder out of fifty had as many as three hearths. Of eight families with two hearths, three were rated as poor; of forty-one families with a single hearth thirty-one were poor. No fewer than 68% of the households of Appleshaw were exempted because of their poverty, as compared with 24% in Thruxton and only 17% in Fyfield. Elementary analysis of this kind reveals important comparative evidence, and forms an excellent basis for more complicated research using sources such as wills, inventories and parochial accounts.

Exercise

Draw up a scheme of analysis for any major source, or group of sources, with which you are familiar. Test it to see what kind of generalisations emerge.

---

[1] See T. L. Stoate, *Cornwall Hearth and Poll Taxes, 1660-4* (Bristol, 1981).

[2] This needs to be put into a wider perspective. Elsewhere in Hampshire, and at the same date, at least three major houses had 50 or more hearths.

Appendix 7

ANALYSIS OF DOCUMENTS — 2

Poor-law examinations record face-to-face interviews between local magistrates and paupers. This class of document has attracted considerable attention in recent years, as a means of illuminating the lives of people who normally created no records for themselves. In particular they frequently describe the employment and family history of each individual: great attention was paid to the time spent in particular jobs and places, so that legal settlement could be properly determined. At their best examinations amount to a kind of biography or even autobiography.

SETTLEMENT EXAMINATION

Transcribed example from P. Hembry, *Calendar of Bradford-on-Avon Settlement Examinations and Removal Orders, 1725-98* (Wiltshire Record Soc., xlvi, 1990), p. 99

'Examination of Henry Gibbs, broadweaver, now in Frome (Frome Selwood), Somerset, before William Jones and Thomas Coward the younger (1 March 1758). 42 years old. Born in Warminster, where he lived until he was eight years old. Was then apprenticed by the parish officers there to John Self, broadweaver, of Bradford, with whom he lived nearly four years. Self, failing in trade, assigned him to Jeremiah Cooper, broadweaver, of Bradford for the remainder of the apprenticeship. Lived with and served Cooper as his apprentice for about seven years, then eloped to Horningsham, where he worked as a journeyman broadweaver at the wages of 3d. out of every 1s. for about 12 months. Then he returned to Warminster where an agreement was made by his brother with Thomas Webb, clothworker, for him to serve Webb for three years at the wages of 2s.6d. a week for the first year, 3s.6d. the second and 5s. the third. Served Webb in Warminster for about half a year, then returned to Horningsham and worked there as a journeyman broadweaver for about a year and a half more at the wages of 4d. out of 1s. Then he went to Frome and agreed to serve Simeon Ayres, broadweaver, there for a year at the wages of £3 and meat, drink, washing and lodging. Lived with and served Ayres in Frome from within two or three days of the feast of St James until a fortnight or three weeks after Christmas. Then Simeon

Ayres and he consenting that the said agreement should be void, he worked as a journeyman broadweaver for Ayres at the wages of 3½d. out of 1s. until the next Lady Day. He continued to work as a journeyman broadweaver for Simeon Ayres and other persons in Frome until about three weeks ago, except about two years during which he kept a loom and was a master broadweaver. Has a wife, Mary, living and two children, Mary three years and more and Sarah one year and three quarters.' [*Mark of Henry Gibbs*]

Although variable in length and content, examinations usually contain the same categories of information. If therefore a large number is being studied, for example for a particular parish or district, or for members of a particular occupation such as weavers or sailors, they are certainly worth analysing in a systematic and comparative way. The following is a list of headings which seem to capture the normal contents, and which could be used as the basis of a card-index or computerised spread-sheet. Clearly the information divides into several broad categories, as shown below, and the amount of space finally allotted to each item will vary considerably. One's final layout may well depend on some preliminary experimenting.

1.   Number of Case/Reference
2.   Date of Examination
3.   Names of Justice(s)

PAUPER
4.   Name
5.   Residence of Pauper
6.   Occupation(s) of Pauper
7.   Age of Pauper
8.   Birthplace of Pauper
9.   Settlement of Pauper

PARENTS
10.   Names
11.   Settlement of Parent(s)

SPOUSE AND CHILDREN
(NB: more than one spouse may be mentioned)
12.   Name
13.   Settlement of Spouse
14.   Date of Marriage
15.   Names & Ages of Children

APPRENTICESHIP
16.   Payer of Premium
17.   Name(s) of Master(s)
18.   Trade(s) of Master(s)

19.   Residence of Master(s)
20.   Length of Term Served
21.   Wages/Conditions of Service

_____

OTHER EMPLOYMENTS
22.   Name(s) of Master(s)
23.   Trade of Master(s)
24.   Residence of Master(s)
25.   Place(s) of Employment
26.   Wages/Conditions
27.   Service in Army/Navy

_____

PROPERTY
28.   Ownerships
29.   Renting

_____

OTHER INFORMATION
30.   ?literacy
      ?education
      ?religious affiliations
      etc.

_____

Appendix 8

ANALYSIS OF DOCUMENTS — 3

The last two examples were concerned with sources which were fairly repetitive in character. Certainly any large-scale source such as a tax-list or a bundle of poor-law papers can be profitably analysed on its own account. However, historians frequently commit themselves to more complicated analysis by extracting and *assembling* evidence from a variety of very different sources. They do this in the hope of building up a fuller and more detailed picture of the past, even though further complications and inconsistencies may arise. A good example can be seen in the process known as 'nominal record linkage' by which all the available evidence for particular historical individuals and families is brought together and recorded in a systematic way.

The table opposite comes from the work of a local historian who is concerned with the demographic and social history of Long Melford in Suffolk: she has devised this computerised 'form' in order to record the history of individual marriages and families. The sources include parish registers, wills, inventories, churchwardens' accounts, overseers' accounts, tax lists, ecclesiastical visitations and tithe books.[1]

---

[1] I am grateful to Lyn Boothman of Cambridge for permission to use this table.

Surname	Smith			
Husname	William			
Husbap	2/12/1599			
Husbur	4/5/1668			
Wifenee	Aggas			
Wifname	Rachell			
Wifbap	22/10/1605			
Wifbur	24/4/1670			
Datemar				
Datend	4/5/1668			
Datenext				
Child1	S	Roger	25/2/1624	bur 1676
Child2	S	William	12/9/1625	marr by 1648, Katherine, bur 1667
Child3	D	Mary	14/10/1628	marr to John Smyth of Pakenham, alive 1668 with c
Child4	D	Rachell	9/2/1631	bur 12/1/1635
Child5	D	Ane	14/1/1633	marr John Hayward pre 1664, alive 1669
Child6	D	Rachell	17/12/1639	marr Philip Garwood, alive 1668; prob outside Melford
Child7	S	Thomas	29/7/1649	alive in 1676; marr 1671 Mary Goulden prob
Child8				
Child9				
Child10				
Child11				
Child12				
Details	1624-28	William churchwarden		
	1634	William churchwarden		
	1637	in will of Roger Aggas children are mentioned and Rachell his daughter left money and silver		
	1638	two Williams on Able Men of Suffolk listing		
	1639	Ann Aggas sister of Rachell leaves her children money in her will. William S is exec		
	1644	in will of Rachell Aggas her daughter Rachell is left a tenement and grandchildren get gold rings and other goods and money		
	1647	William the butcher, son of Thomas Smith als Boston, pays £1 11s tithe. Def this one		
	1652	William exec of his mother's will, she mentions Rachell; leaves him £20		
	1666	Mary Lambert, Rachell's sister, leaves William Smith 'my messuage and tenement called Bares ... in his occupation' on condition that he sells it to pay her legacies and debts. William is exec of her will. Mary also leaves money to Roger, Mary, William and their families.		
	1668	William a butcher by his will, as was his son William		
	1668	William's inventory totals £301 9s 6d of which £54 8s 10d household goods. Includes cattle horses pigs and farm implements.		
	1669	Rachell writes her will, Rachel snr. wid. Thomas Smyth and Philip Garwood her execs, superv Thos Hobart		
	1670	Rachel's inventory value £108 14s 0d of which household goods £53 16s 4d. Furniture plus 6 cows, 2 hogs, subtithe and corn on the ground, £70 5s 0d cash to hand		
	1674	Roger's will mentions his brother Thomas and 'Philip Hamond my brother in Sudbury'		
Husfath	Thomas Smith/Boston d1625			
Husmoth	Mary nee Frend d1651			
Wiffath	Roger Aggas d1637			
Wifmoth	Rachell nee Goulding			

The Smith Family of Long Melford, Suffolk, 17th Century: Computerised Analysis from Multiple Sources

Appendix 9

ANALYSIS OF DOCUMENTS — 4

Until recently, probate accounts (as opposed to wills and inventories) were a relatively unexplored historical source. They list the income and expenditure of both executors and administrators of wills, often over years, and contain a wide range of information on, for example, funerals, board and lodging, travel, debts, the education of children, and clothing. Recent research on probate accounts surviving for several English counties, from the late 16th century to 1700, has led to the compiling of a large computerised database. The section dealing with clothing is particularly detailed and contains as many as 27 different columns of information. It throws light on contemporary dress, almost always for children of the deceased testator. The social range is generally 'middling' but wide, below the level of gentry and above that of wage-labourers.[1] The computer can of course sort this information in many different ways, for instance by type of clothing, by county, by price, and by date. The table below, derived from the original database, concentrates on *hats* and is sub-divided by county.[2] Some children appear more than once because the relevant probate accounts cover several years.

---

[1] The program used for the database was Excel; the information was later transferred into Access for sorting and tabulating.

[2] This table is reproduced here by kind permission of Prof. Margaret Spufford, and with the help of Sue Stearn and Nesta Evans. The database of all probate accounts is held in the Literary and Language Computing Dept at Cambridge, and is in effect an index to their contents.

01-Apr-98

Cost of hats analysed by county

Kent (continued)

489	Anne	Russell	hatt	0	1	6
429	Julian	Doyse	hatt	0	1	8
495	Richard	Craft	hatt	0	2	6
495	Richard	Craft	hatt	0	2	8
495	Richard	Craft	hatt with a feather	0	3	0
511	Martha	Ellice	hatt	0	4	0
501	William	Huckstep hatt		0	2	0
569	Thomas	Woode	hate	0	1	8
501	Thomas	Huckstep hatt		0	1	4

Lancashire

Record	Child's name		Description	£	Cost s	d
644	Elizabeth	Jackson	hatt and band	0	3	1
651	Thomas	Heyward	hatt	0	0	0
646	Margaret	Hey al. Harrison	one flower to sett in her hatt	0	0	1
650	Gabriel	Butler	hatt	0	0	0
649	Abraham	Butterworth	hatte	0	2	4
649	John	Butterworth	hatte	0	2	8
647	Isabel	Cooke	hatt for her wedding	0	9	6
646	Margaret	Hey al. Harrison	hatt	0	0	0
644	Margery	Jackson	hatt	0	0	0
644	Margery	Jackson	hatt	0	0	0
644	Margery	Jackson	hatt and band	0	1	8
644	Elizabeth	Jackson	hatt	0	0	0
649	John	Butterworth	hatte	0	2	2

Lincs

Record	Child's name		Description	£	Cost s	d
62	Richard	Allam	hat	0	2	0
15	William	Dowse	hatt	0	2	0
59	Sarah	Wabbut	straw hatt	0	1	3
72	John	Darwin	a new hatt	0	5	0
66	Mathew	Richardson	a hatt	0	1	6
11	John	Barnes	hatt	0	3	4
62	Richard	Allam	hat	0	1	8
15	Robert	Dowse	hatt	0	1	5
43	Joseph	Webdale	a hatt	0	1	4
25	John	Harrison	hat	0	3	4
42	Edward	Tuffine	a hatt	0	4	6
42	George	Tuffine	a hatt	0	3	0
56	Sarah	Chaire	hatt	0	1	2
54	Thomas	Whalepoole	a hatt	0	2	3
43	Thomas	Webdale	a hatt	0	2	6
53	Robert	Schochie	hatt	0	2	10
53	Robert	Schochie	hatt	0	3	3
47	Richard	Etherington	a hatt	0	4	6
52	James	Stevens	a hatt	0	1	10
59	Joanna	Wabbut	straw hatt	0	1	3
36	Rebecca	Chapman	a hatt	0	4	0
49	John	Dinsdale	one hatt	0	3	0
37	John	Wood	a hatt	0	3	10
54	Jonathan	Whalepoole	a hatt	0	2	1

Somerset

Record	Child's name		Description	£	Cost s	d
8	Henry	Isgar	a hat	0	1	0
5	John	Holloway	hat	0	3	0

Probate Accounts: Computerised Analysis

Appendix 10

SHAPE IN WRITING: AN ANALYSIS

The purpose of this appendix is to show how a piece of history is constructed around a basic framework of ideas. It makes use of an article published in *The Local Historian* of November 1996 (Vol.26, No.4), entitled '**Long-Distance Migrants and Cultural Identity: The Example of a Welsh Colony in South Yorkshire'**. Written by Melvyn Jones of Sheffield Hallam University (who has a strong family connection with the subject), this is an appealing study of a group of Welsh people who migrated to a pit-village in south Yorkshire, after their mine in north-east Wales was irrecoverably flooded in 1884. Although the main focus is on a single mining community in the late 19th and 20th centuries, the article has genuine regional dimensions and raises questions which could be applied to industrial communities in other parts of the country.

The article is divided into six titled sections, which immediately give a thematic and chronological structure. They are:

[Introduction]
Disaster
'The Scattering of the People'
The South Yorkshire Colony: Foundation, 1884-1891
The South Yorkshire Colony: Consolidation, 1891-1902
The South Yorkshire Colony: Maturity and Decline, 1902-1984

What follows is not a critique of the quality of Jones's writing or research, but an attempt to summarise how he planned his text; it draws attention to the principal ideas and questions which lie inside the article. This is the kind of deliberate design that should lie inside any piece of historical writing, and which is essentially similar to the skeleton plan which writers are recommended to produce as a preliminary to writing (Appendix 11, pp. 121-2). In the article proper, each point is fleshed out with considerably more detail than is suggested here, and references are made to the research of other historians.

Introduction
* In the second half of the 19th century, migrants contributed significantly to the rapid growth of the south Yorkshire coalfield.

- Most of new migrants were Yorkshire-born, and had come only short distances.
- But has the importance of longer-distance migration been under-emphasised?
- The purpose of this article to test this possibility in relation to the village of Carlton, near Barnsley in south Yorkshire.

Disaster
- Quay Colliery at Mostyn on Welsh side of Dee estuary: the estuary broke into the mine on 19 July 1884.
- 200 men and boys lost employment; attempts to pump out mine failed. (Quotation from *Flintshire Observer*, 24 July 1884.)

'The Scattering of the People'
- Devastating impact of the flood: unemployment and population decline.
- Importance of unique document written by a collier in 1889, describing the effect on over 100 families or individuals.
- Migration often happened in stages: the young going first, seeking new employment, and heads of households later.
- Women and children left last. Some kept their homes at Mostyn after migration: example of Gittins family.
- Bad effect on local businesses and cultural life of Mostyn.
- Miners of Mostyn preferred to stay in same occupation, even if it meant moving home. Some went to other collieries in North Wales, which were short-lived. A number eventually found employment at the Point of Ayr Colliery (north of Mostyn) which reopened in 1885.
- Others migrated to various parts of Wales and England, or went overseas (map).
- By Easter 1889, 170 former residents of Mostyn were living in England, mostly in the Lancashire coalfield. A few in north Staffordshire and south Yorkshire.

The South Yorkshire Colony: Foundation, 1884-1891
- Crucial significance of Evan Parry, native of Mostyn: in Nov. 1884 appointed manager of Wharncliffe Woodmoor Colliery at Carlton near Barnsley.
- In 1884 Parry was 37; his household consisted of wife, 4 children and widowed mother. Other members of his own family followed them.
- Other pioneering Welsh families arrived: Jones, Hodgson, Macdonald, etc.
- Thirteen lodgers of North Welsh origin at Carlton in 1891 census: some later became prominent in Welsh community.

The South Yorkshire Colony: Consolidation, 1891-1902
- Welsh community at first dispersed in both Carlton and district around: need to rent accommodation where available.

- In 1891 Parry bought Brookfield House and land on Chapel Lane in Carlton; he built 22 new houses (map).
- Need for place of worship for Welsh speakers in Calvinistic Methodist tradition. Welsh church founded in summer of 1890; had no permanent home for several years.
- Benjamin Francis became popular visiting preacher; in 1900 he became pastor of a 'free church' with 43 members.
- Campaign to create a Welsh chapel in 1901; building fund supported by donations and special concerts; site leased in Carlton Lane; corrugated-iron chapel opened on 6 June 1902, at cost of £200.

The South Yorkshire Colony: Maturity and Decline, 1902-1984
- More difficult phase to chart, especially for the wider community with Welsh connections. Shortage of evidence, except for chapel itself.
- Highwater mark of Welsh community between opening of chapel in 1902 and First World War. Carlton known as 'Little Wales': Anglo-Welsh community of several hundred. The chapel was of central cultural importance, e.g. singing festivals.
- Welshness progressively diluted by strong forces, educational and social. Some children unable to speak Welsh, only English with Yorkshire accent. Intermarriage with other groups.
- Evan Parry died in 1912, his wife in 1914. He had provided employment and housing, and held various local offices, e.g. parish councillor.
- After First World War, intermarriage continued to weaken the tradition. Yet chapel still prospered; some new migrants from Wales to Barnsley area joined the congregation.
- By 1980s chapel at low ebb: final service in Dec. 1983; demolition in 1984.
- This Welsh community certainly not unique: e.g. other groups in south Yorkshire from West Midlands, Ireland, South Wales and Scotland.
- More research needed into such long-distance migrant communities. Role of employers? How many true pioneers (like Evan Parry)? How much 'chain migration' involving relatives, friends and neighbours? How long did such communities persist? And why? How important was national identity, language and religious allegiance (undoubted factors at Carlton)?

Appendix 11

PRODUCING AN OUTLINE PLAN FOR WRITING

However much time they have spent on pondering their evidence, most authors find that they cannot plunge with confidence into a first draft without creating some sort of plan or skeleton of ideas. This exercise is a way of sketching the main outlines of one's historical argument, deliberately concentrating on broad generalisation rather than fine detail. The length and elaboration of such a plan will vary from individual to individual, though most people will probably want to mention the principal idea behind each successive paragraph. Overleaf is an example from the author's own work: this is the manuscript sketch made for the introduction to a piece of historical editing.[1] The essence of each paragraph was expressed in a few words (not complete sentences). Notice that the notes were not sacrosanct, and that they were modified and expanded as the first draft took shape. Items were ticked off as the writing proceeded.

[facsimile overleaf]

---

[1] D. Dymond, *The Register of Thetford Priory*, British Academy & Norfolk Record Soc. (2 vols, 1995-6).

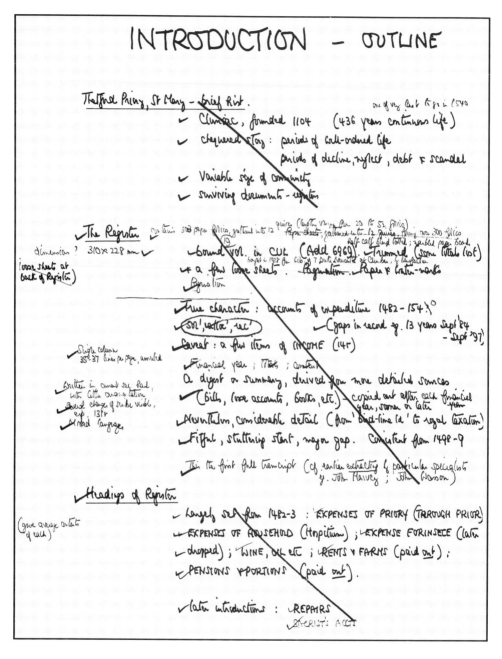

An Outline Plan for Writing: Facsimile

Appendix 12

CHOOSING WORDS

AND FRAMING SENTENCES

The same thought can be expressed in many different ways, and the challenge of writing is to find a form which is clear, concise and dignified. As an example a single sentence has been chosen from an article published in a national journal in 1992. The place-name has been altered for diplomatic reasons:

'It would appear that the age at marriage of the Borchester nonconformists was not markedly different from their Anglican-marrying counterparts.'

Wordy and lumpy in style, this is fairly typical of modern academic writing. Notice the oblique impersonal opening, and the use of a place-name as adjective. The phrase 'Anglican-marrying counterparts' is not only ungainly and impersonal, but is actually ambiguous. It could imply, though unlikely, that the so-called 'counterparts' were people of *other* religious persuasions who were marrying Anglicans. By re-thinking the elements in this sentence, we can soon improve it. Each variant below is better than the original but the fifth, with a strong verb and simple directness, omits nothing and is probably the best.

Alternative versions:

1. 'The age of marriage for Borchester's nonconformists was roughly the same as for its Anglicans.'
2. 'In Borchester nonconformists married at approximately the same age as their Anglican neighbours.'
    [The verb 'married' is stronger than the original 'was'.]
3. 'The age at which nonconformists married in Borchester did not differ markedly from that of Anglicans.'
    [This introduces a new verbal emphasis.]
4. 'Borchester's nonconformists married at roughly the same age as its Anglicans.'
5. 'Nonconformists in Borchester married at roughly the same age as Anglicans.'
    [The word 'roughly' carries the element of doubt which appeared in two places in the original.]

NOTE: later revision, which all writers must be prepared to do, often necessitates the fundamental re-thinking and re-working of individual sentences.

Appendix 13

CHARACTERISTICS OF

HISTORICAL LANGUAGE

The following is a tongue-in-cheek attempt to list words and phrases which seem commonplace in historical writing. In all seriousness one can neither recommend nor condemn this kind of language: it results from the historian's expression of complicated thoughts and judgements by a scrupulously careful choice of words — even at the risk of being thought fussy, pedantic and indecisive.

Adverbs: Perhaps ... possibly ... presumably ... conceivably ... arguably ... apparently ... admittedly ... nearly ... almost ... partly ...

Adjectives: Questionable ... plausible ... unproven ... hypothetical ... likely ... reasonable ... misleading ...

Negative expressions: Not improbable ... not a few ... not infrequently ...

Conjunctions: If ... but ... although ... whereas ... yet ... nevertheless ... notwithstanding ... in spite of ...[1]

Words of emphasis: Furthermore ... moreover ... indeed ... in fact ... especially ...

Phrases: It seems that ... it may be ... suggests (implies) that ... one is tempted to say that ... it is a reasonable assumption (hypothesis, interpretation) that ... on balance it would seem ... the balance of opinion probably favours ... the evidence so far as it goes ... the meaning is not altogether clear ... regrettably we are not told ... fragmentary though the evidence is ... there is no way of telling ... caution forbids ... it would be hazardous ... our best evidence lies in ... on the one (other) hand ...

The language of reviews: (Un)controlled imagination ... (un)critical ... (un)scholarly ... respect for the truth ... rooted in the evidence ... ill-judged ... axe to grind ... politically prejudiced ... heap of facts ... shift of opinion ... persuasive argument ...

Of course language of this kind can be overused, and often needs pruning at a later stage. In other words, writing can be weakened or paralysed by excessive caution. Indeed, when we have firmly held opinions for which the evidence seems reasonable, we should have the courage to state them boldly — with the minimum of qualification.

---

[1] 'However' is not a conjunction, but is often misused as one: 'It was raining, however I walked home.'

Appendix 14

THE HISTORIAN'S RELATIONSHIP

TO SOURCES

[Note: in the examples which follow, an asterisk marks where a reference is given in the original.]

1. An historian in his writing does not normally summarise the strengths and weaknesses of every document he has used. That would be tedious, and could be an excuse for not writing at a higher, more creative level. Generally, the sources are pushed into the background, and into references, as the historical argument is logically unfolded. If, however, a document (or group of documents) is of really central importance in the research, and poses interesting problems of interpretation, the historian can with effect include a deliberate assessment. For example:

> The main framework of the book is based on new factual evidence from a comprehensive collection of probate inventories from eight parts of England.*
> These listings of movable goods were made by neighbours shortly after a person's death, and the executors or administrators of the estate were required to exhibit the inventory at the time of probate. They were commonly made throughout the seventeenth century and became rare only after the 1720s, although the precise date varies in different dioceses. In them are listed, sometimes in considerable detail, the farming, trade, and household goods of the deceased person, together with cash and debts due. They do not record debts owed or any real estate, so they do not give a complete account of the person's wealth, although they normally give a full account of household contents. They also record other information, notably the date, the parish of residence, and the occupation or status. Each inventory contains some information about factors that may have influenced ownership, with the exception of age at death and details about the size and structure of the household. Thus it is possible to gain a considerable body of information from inventories about who exactly owned domestic goods, especially before 1725.
> (from Lorna Weatherill, *Consumer Behaviour and Material Culture in Britain, 1660-1760* (1988), p. 2)

2. The historian will often find pieces of evidence which are complementary. In other words, the weaknesses of one document may be balanced by the strengths of another. Though problems of interpretation will always arise, this kind of accumulation and cross-fertilisation enables him to build up a more detailed, and therefore more truthful, picture of the past. Thus:

> After the Norman conquest, and more especially in the twelfth, thirteenth and fourteenth centuries, Rochester Bridge [*Kent*] enters recorded history with increasing frequency. The testimony of chronicles and increasingly of records (first those of the cathedral priory of Rochester and then, from the thirteenth century, the chancery enrolments of the various offices of royal government) enable us to fill out the story of the bridge and the constant struggle to maintain it in usable condition. The entry of the bridgework list into the great cartulary of the cathedral priory, the *Textus Roffensis*, in the time of Bishop Ernulf (1115-1125) is itself a reflection of the growing importance of the written word in Anglo-Norman England. We cannot tell whether it had also been occasioned by a recent collapse and repair of some section of the bridge. Only a few years later a general writ-charter of King Henry I in favour of the monks of Rochester confirmed them in possession of all the lands and rights that they had in the reigns of William the Conqueror and of William Rufus: among these rights was specified the fourth penny of tolls by land and water at Rochester and also of ferry dues when the bridge was broken.*
>
> (from N. Yates & J. M. Gibson (eds), *Traffic and Politics: The Construction and Management of Rochester Bridge, AD 43-1993* (Rochester Bridge Trust, 1994), p. 35)

3. The third extract shows in greater detail the practical difficulties of trying to build up an interpretation from two or more sources. Often documents are not dealing with exactly the same categories. The historian who does not appreciate such differences, and allow for them, cannot interweave the evidence to form an acceptable interpretation. In this extract, we see an historian wrestling fairly grimly with difficult sources, in order to wring tentative conclusions from them:

> Detailed examination of the evidence available on the size of Orwell [*Cambs.*] shows just how misleading subsidy returns can be. There were fifty-two taxable individuals there in 1524, and forty-six households, according to the bishop, in 1563. This difference is probably accounted for by the changed basis of assessment, rather than by any real change. Only forty-five houses were recorded by the hearth tax assessors of 1664, however. This was certainly an underestimate, for the names of all the tenants of the manor, both freeholders and copyholders, were listed in 1649, 1650 and 1672. The

numbers recorded were both fairly consistent and static, between fifty-four in 1650 and fifty in 1670 [*sic*]. The map made in the 1670s shows fifty-five houses. There may therefore have been an increase of about a fifth in the number of households between the bishop's estimate in 1563, and the 1670s, always provided that the bishop's figure was accurate. The baptism trends from the parish registers suggest fewer families in Orwell in the 1660s than in the 1570s. However, despite the proven inaccuracy of the hearth tax in this instance, the picture of the overall size of Orwell remains a fairly static one with its fifty-two taxable adults in the 1520s, and its fifty to fifty-four tenants in the 1670s.

(from Margaret Spufford, *Contrasting Communities* (1974), p. 23)

Appendix 15

EXAMPLE OF WRITING,

WITH DETAILED CRITIQUE — 1

The following extract is taken from David Levine & Keith Wrightson, *The Making of an Industrial Society: Whickham, 1560-1765* (1991), a prestigious book dealing with an agricultural-cum-mining parish in County Durham. Although the research behind the study is deep and complex, the writing remains accessible and persuasive. Here the content and style of a single paragraph is analysed in some detail. After each sentence is a comment, in square brackets. An asterisk marks a reference in the original.

[p. 195]

'Closer analysis of the major crises of the early seventeenth century certainly reveals the demographic "footprint" of the plague.'

[This sentence stakes out the subject of the whole paragraph; it also links 'backwards' to the preceding paragraph by using the words 'closer' and 'certainly'.]

'In 1604, most catastrophic of the crisis years, 254 inhabitants of Whickham were buried in only five months, perhaps a quarter or more of the entire population.'

[This generalisation is powerful because it is not obscured by a lot of personal detail (which many writers would add at this point). Yet it is based on extensive research. The number of deaths had to be worked out from 254 entries in a parish register: it is not the kind of fact that simply had to be read in a source and copied. Notice how the number 254, though impressive enough, is made more effective by then putting it differently, as an estimated proportion of total population. Furthermore this particular mortality is emphasised as the worst over a period. Helpfully, the date is placed at the beginning of the sentence.]

'Burials were at their peak in July to September, declining thereafter as winter approached — a seasonal pattern of mortality characteristic of the plague.'

[Extra detail shows that burials were highest in summer and early autumn. This is part of the 'footprint' of plague mentioned in the first sentence. If used sparingly, dashes can be a useful form of punctuation, stronger than commas.]

'Moreover, many deaths were bunched in family units, another familiar feature of epidemic mortality.*'

[The theme is developed further, this time looking at family connections which are also part of the 'footprint'.]

'Of the fifty-one victims of the plague who could be 'placed' in reconstituted families, more than half occurred in family clusters, with mortality worst among infants and young children.*'

[The time-consuming technique of 'family reconstitution' is alluded to: a smaller proportion of families than usual could be reconstructed at Whickham because of the high mobility of its population. This sentence gives more detailed evidence, and confesses its limits, to substantiate the claim that many children died. Notice that throughout this paragraph the word 'plague' has been preceded by an unnecessary 'the'.]

'While some of Whickham's relatively settled families suffered drastically, however, the culling of the parish population seems to have been at its worst among the floating population of sojourners and short-term residents attracted to Whickham by the labour needs of the coal industry.'

[The final distinction is between the 'settled' and 'floating' populations. One wonders whether the word 'however' applies to the first or second part of the sentence.]

'Clearly, the isolated individuals of the migrant population suffered dreadfully.'

[A final short judgement which seems weakened by the rather colloquial 'dreadfully'.]

Appendix 16

EXAMPLE OF WRITING,

WITH DETAILED CRITIQUE — 2

The following extract comes from a parish history published in 1933. Its title is not mentioned here for obvious reasons, for it contains most of the flaws which disfigure historical writing. To put the case bluntly, this is no more than an uncritical rag-bag, very often in the shape of over-long quotations (without references). Although the author consulted local and national sources, and probably read some general books, he made little attempt to use, shape or interpret his information. It is no good quoting an historical fact unless one explains, or debates, its significance.

This boring shapeless piece of prose is of little interest — even to a local resident. Yet such writing is frequently justified by authors and publishers on the grounds that it is designed for local consumption and not for 'academics'. This insults the intelligence of local people, who need properly constructed history as much as anyone else.[1] It is a sad reflection that prose of this kind is probably more common today, because of the greater numbers of people writing and publishing.

Each chunk below is a separate short paragraph in the original. Short paragraphs (often with long sentences) are always a sign of heaped uncritical history. At the end of each paragraph, comments are appended in square brackets.

'The parish constable was elected annually, and occasionally a headborough was mentioned in the accounts. The first direct reference to a parish beadle appears in the Minutes of 17th November, 1770, when John Wicksteed was appointed at a salary of four pounds a year, "time and expenses being extra".'

  [What did the parish constable do? What is the significance of a headborough? We are not told. If it is important for us to know that Wicksteed was paid £4 a year, was it a good or bad wage by contemporary standards?]

'The making of rates was not a popular task, as Mr John Fassett, overseer, found when

---

[1] But let it not be thought that this 'descriptive' or heaping approach to the past is confined to the work of so-called amateurs: it is also a marked feature of many postgraduate theses and can often be found in academic journals.

he called a vestry meeting on 21st May, 1771. No one attended, and so no business could be done. But the money was wanted sadly, and so after waiting two hours, Mr Fassett called upon his brother overseers and churchwardens, and they took the law into their own hands, and levied a rate of one shilling in the pound — two pence for the church and tenpence for the poor.'

[The apathy of the vestry is noteworthy, but again nothing is questioned or explained. Why did the vestry have this attitude, and was it usual? How much money was raised by this rate, and how was it actually spent? Does expenditure vary much over the years?]

'The churchwardens and constable were the only persons present at a vestry held 23rd September, 1771, and they nominated ten gentlemen as parish surveyors, including the parson, under a penalty of one guinea each if they refused.'

[To appoint as many as ten surveyors of highways is not common. And were they all truly 'gentlemen'? What problem with local roads lay behind this interesting decision?]

'At a vestry held at the Gymcrack, April 21st, 1772, six persons attending, it was ordered "That Mr Harradine pay five shillings for a vestry held June 6th, 1771, six shillings for a vestry held September 23rd, 1771, ditto December 5th, 1771, fourteen shillings and threepence, and for this Easter Vestry One Pound three shillings and threepence, halfpence, making in the whole Four Orders £2 8s. 6½d."'

[What a boring quotation! What does it amount to? Was Harradine fined for non-attendance, non-payment of rates, or for some other reason?]

'In an act of Parliament, passed in the reign of William III, "for supplying some Defects in the Laws for the Relief of the Poor of this Kingdom" was made the following enactment: "And to the end that the money was raised only for the relief of such as are as well impotent as poor, may not be misapplied and consumed by the idle, sturdy and disorderly beggars: Be it further enacted by the authority aforesaid … "'

[The quotation continues for another 250 words, and is grotesquely long. The whole extract could have been neatly paraphrased, with perhaps a short and really effective quotation from the original.]

'This Act seems to have been a dead letter in [   ] in this respect, for it was not put into operation until the vestry of 21st April, 1772, when the following was entered on the Minutes:- "It is agreed by this vestry that whoever receives any almens or pencion from this parish shall wear a badge on his or her right sleeve with a P cut in red or blue cloth and two letters for the name of the parish according to an Act of Parliament. Past *neme con*".'

[It is interesting that the 1697 Act, for badging the poor, was still being invoked in 1772. Was there any particular reason? We are clearly meant to be amazed by the quaint spelling.]

Appendix 17

AN EXERCISE IN HISTORICAL WRITING

A Medieval Pilgrimage at Stanton, Suffolk

This is all the significant information known about a minor historical subject which was investigated during the writing of a church-guide. It is given in the order in which it was accidentally found or deliberately looked for. Please absorb the detail with care, and then write your own piece of history. If others have done the same exercise, using exactly the same sources, it can be very instructive to compare results. A specimen draft is provided on pp. 133-4.

1. British Museum, Lansdowne 64, MS 12826: Petition of Richard Sheparde, rector of Stanton, to the Lord High Treasurer, 1590. 'In tyme past the Church called Allsaintes had a Saint called St Parnell standinge in it, wherunto many resorted as Pilgrims and did offer, and therof great gayne was made, which in those daies much holpe the Minister of that Church, and now that lyvinge is much the lesser.'

     NOTE: Parnell is a version of Petronilla. D. H. Farmer's *Oxford Dictionary of Saints* reveals that Petronilla was an early Roman martyr, supposedly the daughter of St Peter, who fasted to death rather than marry a man she despised. The extract above was a chance discovery, based on a reference in W. A. Coppinger, *Suffolk Records and Manuscripts*, v, 26. It immediately raised the question: where can I find more about this cult? Wills and ecclesiastical surveys were possible answers.

2. *Nonarum Inquisitiones* [1340/1], Record Commissioners, 1807, p. 72: 'Item de oblationibus capell' Sancte Petronille virginis vjs. viijd.' *Translation*: 'Also in oblations to the chapel of St Petronilla the Virgin, 6s. 8d.'

3. Suffolk Record Office, Bury St Edmunds [SRO-B], IC500/2/9, f. 135v: will of John Pyke of Stanton, 1451. 'Item lego ad ymaginis[sic] beate Petronille, iiijd.' *Translation*: 'Also I leave to the image of the Blessed Petronilla, 4d.'[1]

4. SRO-B, IC500/2/9, f. 568v: will of Margaret Glover, widow of Stanton, 1474. 'Item lego summo alteri ecclesie sancte Petronille in villa de Stanton predicta

---

[1] The scribe of the will register may have omitted something, because *ymaginis* is in the genitive case. The original could have referred to the making, painting or clothing *of* the image.

pro decimis et oblacionibus meis oblitis, iijs. iiijd.' *Translation*: 'Also I leave to the high altar of the church of St Petronilla in the town of Stanton aforesaid, for my tithes and offerings forgotten, 3s. 4d.'

5. Suffolk Record Office (Ipswich), IC/AA2/1/196: will of Richard Spede of Stanton, 1448. 'Item lego pro picturand' imaginis Beate Marie existentis in capella Beate Petronille, iijs. iiijd.' *Translation*: 'Also I leave for the painting of the image of the Blessed Mary in the chapel of the Blessed Petronilla, 3s. 4d.'

6. Suffolk Record Office (Bury St Edmunds), 574/14: memorandum, 14th century, that certain feoffees intended to provide two wax candles every Sunday and feast day for a year in All Saints' church. 'Unum ante crucificum et alterum ante ymaginem Beate Marie Virginis.' *Translation*: 'one candle before the crucifix and other before the image of the Blessed Virgin Mary'.

7. SRO-B, FL629/4/1: parish register of Stanton All Saints. 'Parnell the wife of Climent Rainer buried', 10 Jan. 1601/2.

8. *Letters and Papers of the Reign of Henry VIII*, vol. 10 [1536], no. 364, p. 144: among the 'vain and fictitious relics' which Drs Layton and Legh noted at Bury Abbey, just before its dissolution in 1539, was the skull of St Petronilla which 'simple folk put on their heads, hoping thereby to be delivered from fever'.

9. Eamon Duffy, *The Stripping of the Altars: Traditional Religion in England, 1400-1580* (Yale, 1992), pp. 167-9: describes minor pilgrimage cults in the later Middle Ages centred on images rather than relics.

10. Architectural evidence: All Saints, Stanton, has three piscinae marking the positions of medieval altars — one in the chancel, one in the cramped north-east corner of the nave where the pulpit now stands, and the third in a spacious and stylish south aisle. The whole church appears to have been rebuilt *c*.1300-20.

A SUGGESTED DRAFT

The Cult of St Petronilla at Stanton

All Saints' in Stanton is an ordinary parish church of no special architectural distinction. One is therefore surprised to learn that it attracted pilgrims for at least 200 years before the Reformation. Richard Sheparde, a rector in Elizabethan times, revealed in a petition to the Lord High Treasurer that 'in tyme past the church called Allsaintes had a Saint called St Parnell [Petronilla] standinge in it, wherunto many resorted as Pilgrims'.[1] So somewhere within this church had been a wooden or stone image of that saint, the daughter of St Peter, which was revered not only in the township of Stanton but from further afield. In addition we know that a special chapel was dedicated to St Petronilla from at least 1340, soon after All Saints was rebuilt in its present form, and that it contained an image of the Virgin Mary as well as one of St Petronilla herself.[2] In support of the chapel, visitors gave offerings and local residents left bequests in their wills. To Margaret Glover, a widow of Stanton who made her will in 1473, St Petronilla was so important that she mistakenly named the whole church after her.[3] This kind of local piety is by no means unusual in the later Middle Ages. All over the country, minor cults sprang up not, as in earlier periods, around the shrines and relics of saints but around particular carved images of them. Their influence was usually quite localised, though in their piety some individual testators left bequests to several such cults in their home districts.[4]

But where, within the church, was St Petronilla's chapel? Three 14th-century piscinae betray the presence of medieval altars: one in the chancel, one in the cramped north-eastern corner of the nave, and the third in the south aisle. As the high altar was dedicated to All Saints and the nave altar could never have been within a chapel, St Petronilla's chapel can presumably be placed at the east end of the spacious and stylish south aisle. In all probability her image, condemned as idolatrous, was destroyed at some point in the 1530s or '40s. Her more famous skull which 'simple folk put on their heads hoping thereby to be delivered from fever' was kept ten miles away at Bury Abbey, but must also have perished when the abbey was dissolved in 1539.[5] In spite of such losses, however, reminders of the old ways and 'superstitions' could linger on for generations in the new Protestant world. In January 1602 the register of All Saints records the burial of the wife of Clement Rainer: her Christian name was 'Parnell'.[6]

References

[1] BM, Lansdowne 64, MS 12826.

[2] *Nonarum Inquisitiones* (1807), p. 72; also the will of Richard Spede of Stanton, 1448 (SRO-I: IC/AA2/1/196).

[3] Will of John Pyke of Stanton, 1451 (SRO-B: IC500/2/9, f. 135v); will of Margaret Glover of Stanton, 1474 (IC500/2/9, f. 568v); memorandum for provision of wax candles, 14th century (SRO-B: 574/14).

[4] E. Duffy, *The Stripping of the Altars* (1992), pp. 167-9. Testators such as Christopher Benytt of Debenham (died 1477) and John Moore of Gislingham (died 1493) left bequests not only to major, long-established cults like St Thomas of Canterbury and Our Lady of Walsingham but also to several more localised cult-images including Our Lady of Woolpit, St Mary of Grace in Ipswich, St Nicholas of Tibenham and the roods of Gislingham and Beccles (SRO-I: IC/AA2/2, f. 347)

[5] *Letters & Papers of the Reign of Henry VIII*, vol. 10 [1536], p. 144, no. 364.

[6] SRO-B, FL629/4/1.

Appendix 18

SHORT EXTRACTS OF WRITTEN HISTORY

The following are all genuine quotations from various kinds of published local history, but for diplomatic reasons names and references are not given and place-names are disguised. If you had made these statements in a first draft, would you be satisfied? Please comment on these extracts and, if you feel so inclined, re-write them. Some are wordy and repetitious; some are illogical; many are misshapen and badly thought-out. But not all are bad! My own reactions are sometimes given in square brackets after the quotation.[1]

1. 'Such evidence may well suggest that it would be unwise to conclude that …'
    [Such wordy introductory language begs to be pruned or entirely cut out]
2. 'These are the only remaining timber-framed buildings surviving in the street today.'
3. 'Borchester appraisers tended to neglect fuel, and in the 18th century often omitted to include poultry and bees.'
4. 'During the 18th century there is no doubt that there was a massive increase in the provision of land carriage.'
    [The colloquial 'there is', 'there was', etc., is woefully overused in writing, sometimes several times in the same sentence.]
5. 'Time seemed to stand still as every day was filled to the brim with adventures, bike rides, damn building.'
    [Spelling *is* rather important.]
6. 'Within the Church and Parish the Rector and his Churchwardens wielded considerable authority, though the Manor and its Courts still survived.'
    [Capital letters are unnecessarily used by many writers for common nouns.]
7. 'But the enduring resentment of the poor against the New Poor Law was shown by the threatening letters, the animal maiming and the arson which continued to be directed against the local administrators of the poor law even after the new system had been imposed in the region.'
    [The definite article 'the' occurs ten times in this sentence; five are not needed at all.]

---

[1] Here in the first edition, I included this sentence: 'Standards-wise it is to be hoped that this quotation series may have an ongoing benefit effect on the history writing situation.' Subsequently I received several critical letters from readers who had not seen the joke.

8. 'I heard about this from John Major whom I bumped into in the street.'

    [Not an ideal form of referencing. Note the ugly effect of 'into in'.]

9. 'The potential of the study of faeces was first realised at the Lloyds Bank site where an object described in the academic report as "a single elongate fusiform mass of organic debris, concreted by mineral deposition", and more commonly known as "the Lloyds Bank turd", was found.'

    [This amusing sentence which pokes fun at academic pomposity, ends weakly with the words 'was found' instead of the climactic word 'turd'!]

10. 'Although brick was used increasingly in Borchester for walling, roofs, floors and occasionally internal partitions were made of timber.'

    [Punctuation can confuse as well as clarify.]

11. 'Its semi-ruinous state is now happily being restored by a new owner.'

12. 'St Agatha's church stands on a downward slope overlooking the valley.'

13. 'A property with a heavily disguised frontage ...'

14. 'The total population was 896 in 1861 excluding those working in the workhouse with an equal distribution of the sexes.'

15. 'Nothing is known of the past landscapes without their historical features, which explain records in maps and documents and are valuable for wildlife.'

16. 'Householders not having gained legal settlement in Ambridge, or who could not prove their financial independence, out-migrated.'

17. ' ... outdoor space was not gendered at this date ...'

    [Ugly and imprecise jargon, meaning that 'at this date women were not unduly restricted in their outdoor movements'.]

18. 'The effect of offspring on the mobility of the family heads was for persistency to increase with the number of resident offspring.'

    [Demographic history often attracts jargon and bad, noun-laden writing.]

19. 'Recent medical research, on the other hand, has introduced the possibility that a sagging age-specific marital fertility curve might equally well be caused by undernourishment: which can both inhibit ovulation and increase the incidence of miscarriage.'

    [An excellent example of divorcing words which should be adjacent or very close: 'sagging' refers to 'curve'.]

20. 'Distance decay in marriage horizons was found, but not in a straightforward sense.'

21. 'It was suggested that one of the reasons why fertility was concentrated into the earlier years of marriage had to do with the comparatively unfavourable mortality experience of first-born children.'

22. 'Such a figure [of illegitimate births] might strike modern readers as rather high, accustomed as they are to present-day contraceptive devices and a view of the past coloured by Victorian prurience.'

    [Notice the amazing use of the word 'prurience' when 'prudery' was intended.]

23. 'In May Council approved the final report on the Churches Plans Index pilot project.'

    [Five nouns in a row.]

24. ' … personal qualities such as people skills …'

25. 'We are striving to attain student enrichment values and to avoid information overload anxiety.'

    [A classic example of transatlantic writing at its worst.]

26. 'Socio-economic change and the loss of spiritual incentives for parish harmony had reinforced existing internal polarization.'

    [An important observation spoilt by impersonal and de-humanized writing.]

27. 'The entry of key sources into databases, both flat file and relational, with text encoding, hypertext or similar, facilitates their use for multiple research purposes.'

    [Dull, ponderous language typical of the new computerised history. Such writers genuinely want to make converts, yet they often have the opposite effect.]

28. 'The appreciable dilution of proprietorial control meant an increasing tempo in the numbers of directors.'

29. 'Much nearer can be seen fine churches at Ambridge and Penny Hassett, whilst in Borchester we have St Julian's church, the oldest ecclesiastical site in the town, dating back to the 7th century the mother church of Borchester, much of it rebuilt by William of Borchester, the 30th Archbishop of Canterbury, founder of Borchester College whose head is preserved in the vestry.'

    [A sad piece of writing, jumbled and not properly thought-out. It could form the basis of at least three separate sentences.]

30. 'The tower built of flint, stone and some brick, began to lean between the two World Wars.'

31. 'When looking at these churches, scattered under the enormous Norfolk sky, and pondering all they represent, one thinks inevitably of the succession of incumbents who ministered in them; the tranquil and unperturbed careers of some, the struggles of conscience and conviction which were forced upon others in the recurrent storms of our ecclesiastical history. At any of the great crises of the church, who was tending his flock in the shadow of each soaring grey tower, who knelt at the altar, whose words were echoed by the sounding-board of the pulpit? Devotee, fanatic or time-server? Wyclifite, Reformer, Marian, Elizabethan, Puritan, Laudian, Non-Juror?'

    [Written between the two world wars by a gentleman-scholar, this extract is too self-indulgent by modern standards, but has great literary quality and humanity.]

32. 'A habit of twenty years or so could be convincingly designated "immemorial custom".'

    [How welcome is a touch of dry humour.]

33. 'Our ignorance is always greater than our knowledge.'

34. 'And when we are served statistics deliciously cooked we are wise to scatter over them the herbs and spices of imaginative literature very finely ground and sieved.'

35. 'Like soft-bodied creatures of the Paleozoic era that left little trace in the fossil record, the poor who did not come to the formal attention of the law left little or no evidence of their time on earth.'

36. 'The surviving peasantry of Western Europe still shock us with their worn hands and faces, their immeasurable fatigue.'

   [A beautiful sentence: the slight pause demanded by the comma has an almost musical effect.]

Appendix 19

LONGER EXTRACTS OF WRITTEN HISTORY

All historical writing is in the last resort unique. Two people may use the same evidence, but the total blend of information and interpretation, and the style by which an historical argument is expressed, can never be repeated — even by the same writer at a later date.

Given that writing reveals more about a person's mind than any other activity, and survives its creator, it is astonishing that so much careless and uncritical work is written and published. In order to show the value of careful thought and style, this appendix gives extracts, generally one to three paragraphs, from the work of eleven historians. Before each extract, a few comments are given in square brackets. Asterisks mark where references are given in the original.

1. Peter Bigmore, *The Bedfordshire and Huntingdonshire Landscape* (Hodder & Stoughton, 1979), p. 21

[In all kinds of writing, the opening paragraph should create interest and have impact. It may not be possible to achieve this at a first attempt. In fact, authors often return to the opening when the book or article is substantially finished.]

'The charms of Bedfordshire and Huntingdonshire draw few visitors from beyond their boundaries and yet the number of people who pass through, by road and rail, must be as great as for any other county within the southern half of England. The two counties lie astride some of the most important long-distance north-south routes: the M1, the A1 and the main-line railways from London to Edinburgh, Leeds, Sheffield and Nottingham daily carry thousands through a landscape that one suspects few will give a second glance. They might well recall an industrial scene, the towering chimneys of the brickworks south of Bedford and Peterborough and the acrid smell of the brick firing that pervades the atmosphere for miles around. Or it might be the sight of intensive market-garden cultivation in eastern Bedfordshire, a scene which at the right time of year might also be recognised by a distinctive smell, that produced by thousands of acres of brussel sprouts!'

2. Steven Runciman, *The Fall of Constantinople, 1453* (CUP, 1965), p. 147

[The following paragraph from a classic book describes an horrific human tragedy, how the great Byzantine church of Haghia Sophia was despoiled in 1453 by Turkish solders who had just smashed through the ancient defences of Constantinople. Written with economy and clarity, it is offered here as an example of narrative history at its best. Notice in particular the value of varying the length of sentences: the shorter ones are especially powerful.]

'The church was still thronged. The Holy Liturgy was ended, and the service of matins was being sung. At the sound of the tumult outside the huge bronze gates of the building were closed. Inside the congregation prayed for the miracle that alone could save them. They prayed in vain. It was not long before the doors were battered down. The worshippers were trapped. A few of the ancient and infirm were killed on the spot; but most of them were tied or chained together. Veils and scarves were torn off the women to serve as ropes. Many of the lovelier maidens and youths and many of the richer-clad nobles were almost torn to death as their captors quarrelled over them. Soon a long procession of ill-assorted little groups of men and women bound tightly together was being dragged to the soldiers' bivouacs, there to be fought over once again. The priests went on chanting at the altar till they too were taken. But at the last moment, so the faithful believed, a few of them snatched up the holiest vessels and moved to the southern wall of the sanctuary. It opened for them and closed behind them; and there they will remain until the sacred edifice becomes a church once more.*'

3. W. G. Hoskins, *The Midland Peasant* (Macmillan, 1957), pp. 278-9.

[Hoskins's writing has an easy elegance which no doubt conceals a lot of hard work. The rise of nonconformity in Wigston Magna is convincingly demonstrated, first by the use of total figures and then by percentages. Throughout we are never in any doubt that figures mean people. Notice the value of imaginative phrases like 'flourished obscurely', 'loud defiant singing' and 'empty Sunday streets'. Characteristically too, this paragraph contains some of Hoskins' personal attitudes and prejudices, for example his sympathy with underdogs and distrust of 'masters'.]

'The church was too closely linked with the masters in the nineteenth century: the wage-earners filled the chapels. Non-conformity had grown strong in Wigston all through the Georgian era. The return made to Parliament in 1829 revealed 520 Independents, 195 Wesleyan Methodists, 105 Primitive Methodists, and 30 General Baptists — a total of 850 nonconformists out of about 2100 inhabitants. In 1676 they had been about 4 per cent of the total population; by the 1720's about 16 per cent;

and a hundred years later they were fully 40 per cent. Their strength had continued to increase in the mid-Victorian decades. The Wesleyans had put up a new chapel in 1839. Two years later the Independents had rebuilt and enlarged their attractive old Georgian meeting-place (first built in 1731), and in 1845 the Primitive Methodists blossomed forth in a new chapel. Here and there in odd corners behind the main streets, other little sects flourished obscurely, worshipping the Almighty in their own way in bare brick tabernacles as ugly as their own cottages. So in 1870 the empty Sunday streets would suddenly resound with the loud defiant singing of the chapels from one end of the village to the other, while from the parish church came the more subdued murmur of "the Conservative Party at prayer".'

4. David G. Shaw, *The Creation of a Community: the City of Wells in the Middle Ages* **(Oxford, 1993), pp. 48-9.**

[Although this extract is full of details such as dates and sums of money, it presents a clear picture of late-medieval urban decay. Sentences are generally short. The first paragraph gives a memorable account of a particular street, which was developed and then disappeared within a century and a half: the significance of detail is always made obvious within an overall argument. The second paragraph is broader in its approach, showing that Moniers Lane was part of a wider picture. It could be criticised for noun-crunching, e.g. 'a High Street toft' and 'A 1592 example', and perhaps for over-labouring the significance of the word 'toft'. The last sentence is a good, powerful climax.]

'The evidence of urban dilapidation is striking, if sometimes difficult to date.* Perhaps the most notable instance of dilapidation in Wells is the history of Moniers Lane. This street was developed in the 1340s, first through piecemeal acquisition, by the merchant Peter Moniers. He acquired enough properties in the block between Sadler Street and Grope Lane to create the new lane in about 1343. He left it to his wife when he died in the early 1350s.* Strikingly, it continued to thrive in the 1350s, and was sold for £133 6s. 8d. in 1369, coming into the cathedral's hands.* At that time it was covered by houses, a bakery and its appurtenances, and a cottage. But in 1425 part of the lane was let as a toft, an empty plot, to which there had been no earlier reference, and nearly 100 feet, or one-third of the lane, were let to Thomas Frome in the same year as a garden, worth only a shilling.* By the 1460s and 1470s the lane had only two houses upon it and was mainly tofts and gardens.* Subsequently, the street entirely disappeared. Moniers Lane prospered even in the wake of the plague crisis, presumably riding a wave of post-plague immigration. It succumbed to some other malaise at the beginning of the fifteenth century.* It is clear, then, that much of the topographical contraction was due to the plague, from which there must have been at least partial recovery.

By the first quarter of the fifteenth century tofts — decayed, unused building sites — were numerous in all parts of the town. In Wells and most urban usages the term "toft" or "toftum" meant a building site, the site of a house.* The *Oxford English Dictionary*'s examples also indicate that it referred to the piece of land, not the physical house. In *rural* circumstances it could mean an entire homestead, but in a town it usually meant a piece of land where a house or building had once stood. A 1592 example is decisive for us: "A toft is the place wherein a messuage hath stand".* The toft implies extreme decay, an empty site. Many of our examples below will unequivocally bear out this definition. But for the present there is the Southover toft which was yielding 16*d.* to the town in 1427-8, but which property had once returned 9*s.* per annum.* No streets were spared the existence of empty, unproductive space. In 1423 the town let a Grope Lane toft to Richard Dyer, and it sat between a privately owned toft and a tenement.* In 1433 Thomas Sholer rented a High Street toft, as did William Beaufitz in 1438.* The empty spaces were universal, no street was without them, and the High Street was particularly affected.'

5. Alan Everitt, *Continuity and Colonization: The Evolution of Kentish Settlement* (Leicester, 1986), pp. 268-9.

[One of the pioneers of English local history here wrestles with difficult evidence, mostly topographical. In the first paragraph he talks of the long droveways running north-south across Kent. In the second and much longer paragraph he develops the theme in greater detail by discussing the relationship between one such droveway and the market-town of Sevenoaks. Various individual pieces of evidence are introduced, but only to support the writer's thesis. Note that the language is frequently tentative and judgmental, using phrases like 'tends to confirm' and 'grounds for believing'. Everitt's personal style involves quite long sentences and frequent semi-colons, but the meaning remains clear. Details of the local landscape are, in the original book, properly related to a map.]

'Not all the lanes of Kent have originated as localized forest footpaths, however; many have developed as relatively long-distance droveways between the mother-settlements of the Original Lands and their forest-pastures on the Downs or in the Weald. It is this circumstance, as we saw in Chapter 2, that lies behind their tendency to run across the grain of the country from north to south. The main droveway of the estate based on Otford in West Kent is an instructive example of this kind of development, leading from the Darent valley at Shoreham through Otford itself, across Holmesdale, and then by way of Sevenoaks and Hubbard's Hill to the swine pastures of the Otford Weald in the neighbourhood of Penshurst and Chiddingstone.* The topography of the parish of Sevenoaks in particular sheds a good deal of light on the evolution of this droveway and is worth describing in detail (see map 13).

The origins of Sevenoaks as an urban settlement are not documented, but they probably go back to the later generations of the Old English period. It was not a "primary town" in the sense of an old *caput*; but archaeological evidence indicates a pre-Conquest market at this point, and the fact that this market was a prescriptive or traditional one, and never acquired a formal charter from the crown, tends to confirm its Old English origin. As an outlying Chartland settlement of the Otford estate, Sevenoaks is not actually recorded until the *Textus Roffensis* of the eleventh century; but in the present context its place-name is a particularly suggestive one. In England it is unique; but it has several parallels on the continent, and Dr Margaret Gelling has suggested that names of this type may have a folkloric significance.* The original settlement must have arisen at some noted meeting-place by seven oak trees, and there are grounds for believing that it was the meeting-place of the Hundred of Codsheath.* This was one of the relatively few Kentish hundreds based on a Jutish estate, and its meeting-place must have been situated on heathland, or in other words on the Chart. In addition to Sevenoaks itself, it included the parishes of Shoreham, Otford, Halstead, Kemsing, Seal, Sundridge, Woodlands, and part of Chevening, and the routes leading southwards from these places still converge upon Sevenoaks market place. That this market developed as the commercial centre of the estate is further attested by the fact that it was the main droveway itself — the Otford road and not the London road — that became the High Street and market place of the town, while the London road was a subsidiary track branching off it.* Though Sevenoaks is only 25 miles from the capital, its origins were essentially dictated by the local needs of the estate and its herdsmen in this way, and not by metropolitan impact. The name of the hundred may also help to explain the unusual situation of the town, some 500 feet up on a windswept ridgeway.* The first element of Codsheath has not been satisfactorily explained, but if its earliest recorded form *Godehede* in 1178-9 means "god's heath", it may suggest that Sevenoaks originated not only as a hundredal market but as the centre of heathen worship in the forest outback.* That would go some way towards explaining its own place-name, more-over, with its possible folklore connotation.*'

6. John Chandler, *Endless Street: A History of Salisbury and its People* (Hobnob Press, 1983), 151-2.

[This extract debates an important aspect of 20th-century urban life rarely studied by local historians — the effect of the motor-car. It makes points which most of us have forgotten or never knew, especially about the 1930s. The writing shows a nice balance between generalisation and detail; paragraphs are well shaped, each built around a central idea which is introduced early. Footnotes quote little-used sources such as the chief constable's annual reports, as reported in a local newpaper.

Car-parks are plotted on a map of the city centre. The effect of writing of this quality is to make us think immediately about the same problems elsewhere and nationally.]

'Between 1932 and 1936 the motor car effected a profound change in what might be called the townscape of Salisbury. Much that is now taken for granted in any street scene originated in those five years, and has been only little modified since. The first car park was constructed — on the site of the present coach station — and the first car park charges levied. For the first time a decision was taken to demolish buildings — in Salt Lane — to make way for a car park. The first parking restrictions — in Castle Street — were imposed. The first one-way streets — Fish Row and Butcher Row — were designated. Traffic lights were placed at strategic junctions. Pedestrian crossings made their first appearance. Thirty mile per hour speed limit signs were erected at all the entrances to the city. And the first police patrol car was bought to ensure that they were observed.*

By 1935 the need for controls of this kind had become acute. The occasional mishaps of the early motorist had turned into a trail of injury and destruction. Road accidents occurred in three principal ways. In the countryside a combination of excessive speeds, inattention at junctions and poor road surfaces often spelled disaster. In the city motorists were travelling too fast along the main roads, especially those which had been recently widened and straightened. It was claimed that speeds of 50-60 mph were constantly achieved along the city's most accident-prone highway, Wilton Road. The third cause of accidents was a lack of road sense on the part of cyclists and pedestrians. Cyclists, who accounted for nearly half the casualties in 1934, were particularly vulnerable, and the introduction of speed limits and a highway code in 1935 seems to have made little impression on them. Between 1928 and 1937, when there were fewer than three million motor vehicles in Britain, the annual average number of people killed or injured on Salisbury's roads was 88. Forty years later the equivalent figure, at 209, had more than doubled, but the number of vehicles had increased six-fold over the same period. In 1934 the number of Salisbury casualties exceeded one hundred for the first time, and 1932 recorded the highest number of accidents. Thereafter speed limits, severer penalties and more rigorous policing succeeded in bringing about a reduction. But for those involved every serious road accident is a catastrophe and such statistics were no comfort to the victims caught unawares. As Edith Olivier observed in describing a rather unusual road accident involving an octogenarian lady and a charabanc: "Little did she think that morning, when she left home in the quiet company of a psychological professor that, before night fell, eighteen fried-fish men would be responsible for her sudden death".*

Besides the dramatic effect that the motor car has had on individual Salisbury citizens, it has also brought about a gradual erosion and transformation of the city itself. Because vehicles occupy a great deal more space than pedestrians, whether moving or still, the city has passively undergone a change of scale. The provision of car parks is an example of this change (Figure 25). In 1949 there were about 800 official parking spaces in the city, occupying most of one of the medieval chequers (Salt Lane car park), a large waste area just outside the original city (the present coach station) and three most important open areas of the medieval city, the Market Place, the Cheesemarket and the Coal Market (New Canal). By the early 1960s the Central car park occupied an area immediately west of the city as large as four or more chequers, and was full of cars. By 1970 large parts of three more chequers had become car parks and the number of spaces had quadrupled since the war. The accommodation of 3,000 large metal boxes, although it had been essential for Salisbury's survival as a real city, seems to have upset some indefinable equilibrium, which lay at the heart of Salisbury's character (Plate 33).*'

7. David Underdown, *Fire from Heaven: The Life of an English Town in the Seventeenth Century* (Harper Collins, 1992), 106-7.

[Underdown's smooth and lucid prose conceals very careful design. Notice how the first sentence of each paragraph outlines the theme to be developed. Of course evidence is mentioned and referenced, but the writing is predominantly a reasoned discussion of that evidence and the broad trends which are thereby revealed. One might object that certain expressions are rather too colloquial, such as 'counted for something' and 'anything to go by'.]

'One of the reformers' most striking successes was the enforcement of regular church attendance. That this improvement occurred cannot be simply attributed to the one shilling fine for absence imposed by the Elizabethan statutes. Such fines were regularly collected, and no doubt they helped, but the general pressure for conformity in a town with Dorchester's reputation must also have counted for something. How successful the campaign was can be deduced from the payments made by the churchwardens for bread and wine at communion services. Nothing is known about the frequency of communion services at the other churches, but at Holy Trinity in the year ending at Easter 1620 there were eleven communions. The churchwardens bought sixty-three quarts of wine (usually "Malaga sack") for these eleven communions. This is about average for the decade ending in 1620, but then the quantity of wine bought increases sharply to an average of over a hundred quarts a year, reflecting the increase in the population of the parish. The churchwardens occasionally presented non-communicants to the Blandford court, but the quantity of wine consumed — enough, on average, for six hundred recipients at each communion — suggests that virtually the entire adult population of the parish regularly received the sacrament. The campaign for church attendance had been dramatically successful.*

So, it appears, was the campaign to clean up the townspeople's sexual habits. In Trinity parish, the only one in Dorchester for which reasonably complete records of births, marriages, and deaths have survived, we can chart changes in the frequency of illegitimate births (always carefully listed in the register); and can discover how many brides were pregnant before they got married, by noting the intervals between weddings and the baptisms of first children.

If the experience of Trinity parish is anything to go by, the Dorchester reformers were strikingly successful. After 1600 there was a sharp decline in the illegitimacy rate, and a less immediate but in the end equally striking decline in the proportion of first children born as a result of pre-marital intercourse.* In both respects Dorchester followed the national trend, but in a greatly exaggerated fashion. Over England as a whole bastardy rates had been climbing — arousing the concern of moralists, naturally — throughout Elizabeth's reign. They reached a peak around the end of the sixteenth century, and then began a steady decline. This is precisely what happened in Dorchester. The peak came in 1597-1601, when about 7 per cent of the births were illegitimate. The first decade of the new century was not much better, with a rate of 5 per cent. But after 1611 the rate declined to 2 per cent or even less, reaching the remarkably low figure of less than 0.7 per cent in the ten years beginning in 1626, and rising to only 1.2 per cent in the 1630s. Although Dorchester follows the national trend, it does so with remarkable abruptness. Before 1611 Trinity's illegitimacy rate was *higher* than the national average; in the decade 1611-20 it was less than half, and by the early 1630s less than a quarter, of that average. The transformation, it is hardly necessary to point out, occurred within a few years of John White's arrival in the parish.*'

8. Margaret Spufford, *Poverty Portrayed: Gregory King and the Parish of Eccleshall* (Centre for Local History, Keele University, 1995), pp. 15-17.

[This extract admirably conveys the excitement and complex questioning of historical research. Eccleshall in Staffordshire is a large parish containing a town and twenty rural hamlets. By the judicious use of figures and percentages, Prof. Spufford argues that in the late 17th century this community contained a surprising amount of poverty. Notice the number of references to other places and to other historians: this is a classic example of *comparative* local history. The actual writing could be criticised for repetitions ('on the grounds of poverty' appears four times); for over-reliance on 'I' and 'we'; and for a certain jerkiness and density of style caused by frequent commas and qualifications ('It was poorer, even, than ...')]

'Local historians forget that, if they are working on a microcosm, it is essential to establish its typicality or a-typicality, as a preliminary. The easiest way to do that, in this period, is by comparing the Hearth Taxes: we have already seen that Gregory King regarded them as a swift guide to possible gentility. Contemporary historians are using them in the same way. The latest piece of work to compare places in this way is Keith Wrightson's splendid study of coal-mining Whickham in County Durham.* I reproduce his table (Table 1), with Joan Thirsk's Needwood Forest, and rural Eccleshall added to it. In Dr Wrightson's six rural areas, the proportion of householders exempt from the tax on the grounds of poverty varied from 22 per cent to 34 per cent. All industrial settlements had more of the poor. His own Whickham, with 79 per cent of householders unable to pay, was poorest of all.

We fully expected Eccleshall, mainly pasture and woodland as it was Dr Joan Thirsk's 'Horn and Thorn' country,* to equal or surpass the poorest rural settlement already investigated. But we did not expect the dramatic results we got. Eccleshall was poorer even than Needwood. Eighty-three per cent of its people lived in houses which only had one hearth, or were exempt on the grounds of poverty. We only had the exempt for 1673, the nearest Hearth Tax to Bishop Lloyd's survey in time, for that part of the 'constablewick' of Eccleshall which lay within the parish itself. No less than 53 per cent of houses with one hearth were exempt on the grounds of poverty in this area, and it did not include all the hamlets at all. The hamlets which we knew from later evidence were really poor, and held the squatters in shacks in Greatwood, Fairoak and Wetwood in Croxton and Charnes were not in the constable-wick. However, Gregory King helped us again here. We only had 31 taxable houses in Croxton, which included Greatwood and Fairoak, in the 1673 Hearth Tax: Gregory King noted there were at least 100 houses in Croxton in 1680.* In 1673, we therefore know that only 31 of them, less than a third, were taxable: so in that hamlet at least 69 per cent of the houses were exempt on the grounds of poverty. Rural Eccleshall was then poorer than any other rural area we know about in England in the 1660s and 1670s.* It was poorer, even, than metal-working Birmingham, and only less poverty-stricken than cloth-making Coggleshall, or mining Whickham. What on earth was going on, or perhaps failing to go on, in Eccleshall? Or did we have a series of pasture-farming settlements, full of by-employment and cottage industry, waiting for industrial takeoff?'

9. Charles Phythian-Adams, 'An Agenda for English Local History' in C. Phythian-Adams (ed.), *Societies, Cultures and Kinship, 1580-1850* (Leicester Univ. Press, 1993), pp. 6-7.

[All local historians, professional and part-time, should study the work of con-temporary academic theorists like Phythian-Adams, Marshall and Matthew Johnson.

They make us discuss the nature and limits of local history, the variable nature of local communities, and the need to work comparatively. Unfortunately their message is often blunted by inflated, heavy and obscure writing. The contrast with the lucid writing of earlier authorities like Hoskins and Finberg, when they too were dealing with abstract concepts, is striking.]

'A first step in such a task must therefore be to identify a means of recovering some acceptable simulacrum of what is here meant by social structure over time, so that consistent comparisons may then be made between separate periods. The only such that is both logically justifiable and realistically available, at least over the last two millenia, is represented by the contemporary arrangement of society on the ground. Indeed, when such patterns are conceived in their widest sense, it is difficult to envisage a better surrogate for a changing local social structure as a whole than the spatial geography of social relations, or, in generalized terms, the residential pattern thrown up by each successive generation. Taken together, *in relation to a broadly perceived territory* (insofar as for earlier periods that may even be reconstructed), such a pattern must be regarded as deeply expressive of contemporary social values. More even than that, many features of residential patterns may be used as measures of structural persistence on the one hand, or of a limited *identifiable* time-span for such structural features on the other. Only a few indicators of these various considerations need be given here. The persistence of certain plan-types for domestic buildings over broadly confined periods is expressive of domestic structures and domestic relations over the same time-scales — the hall-house is an obvious example; while the different sizes of tenement plots (let alone any further land attached to them) will furnish some kind of physical matrix within which the social zoning of a settlement, that is not markedly changing its population level over time, may well persist relatively unaltered. The chronology of different types of secular or religious public buildings, where their siting is known, reflects the duration of certain cultural attitudes; adjustments to their plans or furnishing: the timing of cultural shifts. The very form of a settlement and its physical relationship to local resources may be representative of a widespread pattern over a specific region or even a particular chronological phase. The presence, absence or eventually lessening proximity of specialized elite "settlements" (from castles to country houses), of other specialized institutions like monasteries, or of superior housing generally will be crucial to the adjusting spatial realities of power relations at different periods. Above all, the more general density, distribution and hierarchy of settlement in relation both to current communications and transport facilities over a socially definable district and, also, where it may be recovered, to the ever-varying intensity of economic, cultural and kinship links between the places concerned, together represent the ultimate spatial expressions of changing local social structures at ground level.'

10. Bill Goodhand, 'Changes in Rural Life: Welbourn', Chapter 12 of D. R. Mills (ed.), *Twentieth Century Lincolnshire* **(Lincoln, 1989), pp. 344-5**

[This extract comes from a penetrating study of a Lincolnshire village in the 20th century. The actual writing, it must be admitted, is not electrifying. It is a little wordy and dull, incorporating a large number of statistics, but on the other hand it is certainly not ugly or obscure. The importance of this study lies rather in its content: the fact that it poses major questions about life in one village, and therefore about rural life in general. For example, it challenges popular suppositions about rural change and stability, and debates the effects of modern planning decisions. Quite surprising is the fact that Welbourn saw 'less movement in the population in the 1980s than for the period 1920-60', partly because of the frequency with which agricultural labourers formerly moved job and house on 'flittin' day'. We clearly need many more examples of this kind of local history, with the accent on recent or contemporary life.]

'The availability of so much relatively local employment suggests that the community may not have been destabilized. Indeed, in 1974, 64 per cent of Welbourn households had been established there for at least ten years, although only a quarter of household heads claimed to have Welbourn origins. Household heads born within ten miles amounted to 29 per cent, while among the other natives of Lincolnshire 7 per cent had rural origins, and only 10 per cent had been born in Lincoln, a very much smaller proportion than the 26 per cent who came from outside the county. These figures do not support the general view of the outward movement of a local urban population, and lend support to the general impression that rural stability has been enhanced by men remaining as residents in their home localities, although changing their jobs to work outside their parishes, thus counterbalancing "urban incomers". Perhaps not unexpected is the fact that council house tenants have been the most stable element in the population.*

[next paragraph omitted]

Welbourn falls into a middle group of villages, between those with a declining population, and those growing rapidly with the building of large housing estates. This was the result of a planning policy in which Wellingore and Navenby were identified as growth villages for the area from *c.*1950, where "adequate services can be maintained or provided economically and efficiently".* As Welbourn was seen as not satisfying these criteria, growth has been limited to a long-established curtilage, and in 1977 most of the village became a conservation area following pressure from the Parish Council.'

11. Alan Crosby, *The History of Preston Guild* (Lancashire County Books, 1991), p. 241

[The final paragraph of a piece of writing is worth as much careful consideration as the opening. In this account of the occasional celebration known as the Preston Guild, Alan Crosby concludes his story with effective generalisation and a memorable quotation. The prose could have been tightened further by excising words such as 'it was that' in the seventh line.]

'There is no doubt that both post-war Guilds were triumphantly successful — there has never, in the past 250 years, been one which could not be so described. In the records of every Guild in that time observers have expressed the view that the Guild which had just gone would linger forever in the minds of those who had witnessed or experienced it. In 1952, indeed, the *Preston Guardian* somewhat extravagantly claimed that the Guild of that year would "live as long as human memory and, beyond that, the printed record endure". The same editorial went on to try to analyse just why it was that the Guild was so significant, so successful and so perennially popular. Its conclusion is undoubtedly correct: 'It was largely a matter of atmosphere. Every Prestonian said to himself, "This is the Guild — and I am part of it".*'

Appendix 20

BASIC RULES FOR REFERENCING:

FOOTNOTES, ENDNOTES AND

BIBLIOGRAPHIES

Historical publications are frequently marred by inadequate, inconsistent and eccentric referencing, yet the rudiments, which might at first sight seem complicated, are soon mastered with practice. Below is a résumé of the rules which are generally if not universally adopted, *and* of those details which vary according to personal choice or the system demanded by a particular journal or publisher. For the physical character and placing of references, see pp. 76-7.

1. FOR A SINGLE BOOK
For a full reference, give the details in the following order:
* the name of the writer, with initials or forename first
* the full title, however lengthy and sub-divided, in *italics* or <u>underlined</u>
  (the latter instructs a printer or type-setter to use italics.)
* the name of the publisher
  (this is an essential point of identification, although some writers omit it.)
* the place of publication
  (this can be difficult or impossible to quote, because of changes in the nature of publishing; it is not as important as the name of the publisher, and is often omitted by modern writers.)
* the year of publication
  (this essential piece of information is best given in brackets, to avoid confusion with page numbers; the brackets are often shared with the publisher and/or place of publication.)
* page(s) thus: p. 93 *or* pp. 93-5; chapter(s) thus: ch. 4 *or* chs 4-5.
EXAMPLE: Michael A. Williams, *Researching Local History: The Human Journey*, (Longman, 1996), pp. 266-7. (NB: it is acceptable to use initials in place of forenames, thus: M. A. Williams.)

2. FOR A BOOK OF MORE THAN ONE VOLUME

As with a single book except that:

- the total number of volumes is given, after the title
- the number of the relevant volume comes before the date of publication.
- the abbreviations 'p.' and 'pp.' are dropped.

EXAMPLE: *Guide to the Contents of the Public Record Office*, 3 vols (PRO, London, 1963, 1968) ii, 35-41. (Some people would prefer the volume number in large Roman numerals, thus: II, but this is visually heavy.)

3. FOR AN ARTICLE IN A JOURNAL

For a full reference, give the details in the following order:

- the name of the writer
- the title of the article, in single quotation marks
- the title of the journal, italicised
  (titles can be abbreviated, especially with words like *Trans.*, *Hist.*, *Soc.*, etc., but one should not risk misleading the reader. See Appendix 21, pp. 155-7)
- the number of the volume and, if necessary, the part.
  (it is not necessary to use the words 'volume' or 'part', either fully or abbreviated: the relevant numbers will suffice. However, other details such as '4th series' must be retained. Although it is best to give the numbers of volumes in their original form, Arabic numerals are often preferred to Roman because they are more readily intelligible to modern readers and take up less space.)
- the date, in brackets
- page numbers, without the abbreviations 'p.' and 'pp.'

EXAMPLE: N. Goddard, 'A Contrast in Style: An Appreciation of Two Victorian Agricultural Journalists', *Agricultural History Review*, 44, ii (1996), 180-90. (This journal could have be mentioned as *Agric. Hist. Rev.*, and the Roman number could have been Arabic, thus: 44, 2 or 44: 2)

4. FOR AN ARTICLE OR CHAPTER FROM AN EDITED BOOK

As with an article in a journal, except that:

- the title of the article, in single quotation marks, is followed by 'in' (then the name(s) of the editor(s), followed by the abbreviation 'ed.' or 'eds' in round brackets, the title of the book in italics, publisher, date, pages).

EXAMPLE: Evelyn Lord, 'Communities of Common Interest: The Social Landscape of South-East Surrey, 1750-1850' in C. Phythian-Adams (ed.), *Societies, Cultures and Kinship, 1580-1850* (Leicester University Press, 1993), 131-99.

5. FOR THE SHORTENING OF REFERENCES

In certain circumstances, references can be given in shortened form.

- repetitions of the same publications should be abbreviated — so long as the references are not too far apart, and no ambiguity is caused.

EXAMPLE: Williams, *Researching*, p. 5.

- another strategy for repetitions is to use *op. cit.*, *loc. cit.* or *ibid.* (see 'Latin Terms', below).

EXAMPLE: Williams, *op. cit.* (1969), p. 5.

- the effect of appending a bibliography is also to shorten references, as a way of avoiding unnecessary repetition (see 'Bibliographies', below).

6. FOR A MANUSCRIPT SOURCE

The following details are needed:

- a brief description of the source, with some indication of its date.
- the repository, often in abbreviated form (eg. BL for British Library)
- the reference or call number to the individual piece, usually a combination of numbers and letters
- if necessary, the number of a particular page, folio or membrane

EXAMPLE: Extent of the Manor of Writtle, Essex, 1304: PRO, C133/113(1).

NB: some writers, however, would put the description last. The Borthwick Institute at York, for example, insist on this way of referencing.

7. PUNCTUATION IN REFERENCES

must be consistent. With abbreviations, use a full-stop only when the final letter is not the same as that of the whole word, thus: 'ed.' for one editor, but 'eds' for more than one. To make the printed page generally less spotty, it makes sense to minimise the number of full-stops (*OED* and PRO rather than *O.E.D.* and P.R.O.). Whether or not to put a full-stop at the end of each reference is a matter of personal choice. However, complete sentences within notes should certainly end with full-stops.

8. PAGE NUMBERS IN REFERENCES

must also be used consistently. To save space it pays to elide as many figures as possible, for example 34-7, 155-9. However, in the sequence 10-19, one should retain the penultimate figure, thus 12-14, 113-18. After 'p.' or 'pp.', it is normal to leave a space, though you will find publications where the number directly follows the stop.

9. REFERRING TO EDITORS

In a record publication or in an edited collection of articles by different authors, it is normal to distinguish editor(s) by the abbreviation (ed.) or (eds).

10. LATIN TERMS IN REFERENCES

are still commonplace. If they are to be used (many would say that they are best avoided altogether), they must be used accurately, for example:

- *ibid.* (for *ibidem* Latin for 'at the same place'), which is used when a reference repeats the one immediately before, including the page number. This is the Latin term which is most likely to survive, but it must not be confused with *idem* ('the same person') used when more than one work is quoted for the same author.

- *op. cit.* (for *opere citato*, Latin for 'in the work quoted'), which is used when a reference is repeated with a different page number. The previous reference need *not* have been immediately before. Sometimes, *op. cit.* is used in a very irritating way, forcing the reader to look back through scores, even hundreds, of pages to find the original full reference. In such cases, it is far better to repeat the information in abbreviated form, or to give the cross-reference in a bibliography (see below).

EXAMPLE: Hoskins, *op. cit.*, p. 165.

- *loc. cit.* (for *loco citato*, Latin for 'in the place quoted') which is used to avoid repeating the title of a journal or collection of essays. Again, the gap between the two references should not be annoyingly lengthy.

EXAMPLE: Evelyn Lord, 'Communities of Common Interest', *loc. cit.*, pp. 135-7.

- *passim* (Latin for 'in every part') which indicates that the whole of a particular book or article is relevant. It follows a normal reference, and appears instead of a page number.

- *ex inf.* (Latin for 'personal communication from'), is followed by a personal name.

NB. With these Latin terms, it is best to avoid the use of an initial capital letter such as *Op. cit.* or *Ibid*.

BIBLIOGRAPHIES

A substantial piece of written history should include a bibliography, listing all the sources which have been consulted. Items should appear in the following order, with primary sources coming before secondary:

- Manuscripts (by custom, the British Library is given pride of place)
- Printed sources (e.g. produced by record societies)
- Printed books
- Printed articles
- Unpublished works, such as academic theses.

One should quote publications as in ordinary references, except that the author's surname should *precede* his initials or forename.

EXAMPLE: Williams, Michael A., *Researching Local History* (Longman, 1996).

NOTE: the effect of including a bibliography should be to shorten references. Thus, a bibliography may contain: Levine, David & Wrightson, Keith, *The Making of an Industrial Society: Whickham, 1560-1765* (Clarendon Press, Oxford, 1991). Internal footnotes or endnotes may therefore contain no more than: Levine & Wrightson (1991), p. 169.

Appendix 21

ABBREVIATIONS IN

HISTORICAL REFERENCES

In references, words are commonly abbreviated in order to save space but, to avoid misunderstandings, this should be done as consistently as possible. The list below recommends abbreviations for words frequently met by local historians in citing printed and manuscript sources. They are based mainly on the *Oxford Dictionary for Writers and Editors* (1981) and Maney & Smallwood, *The MHRA Style Manual* (1985).[1] A few other words which are often shortened in references have also been included, and are shown un-italicised. Note that where an abbreviation ends with the same letter as the original, a full-stop has not been used.

abbr.	abbreviated, abbreviation
abr.	abridged
Abstr.	*Abstracts*
Acad.	*Academy*
Agrar.	*Agrarian*
Agric.	*Agricultural; Agriculture*
Ann.	*Annals*
Antiq.	*Antiquarian; Antiquary*
app.	appendix
Archaeol.	*Archaeological; Archaeology*
Architect.	*Architectural; Architecture*
Assoc.	*Association*
Bibliog.	*Bibliography*
bk	book
Brit.	*Britain; British*
Bull.	*Bulletin*

[1] In preference to the 'standard list of abbreviated titles of current periodicals' in *Signposts for Archaeological Publication* (Council for British Archaeology, 2nd edn, 1979), Appendix A, pp. 25-31. The latter includes some odd features, including a total lack of punctuation (thus: *J Brit Soc Master Glass Paint*).

Cal.	*Calendar*
cent.	century[1]
ch./chs	chapter/chapters
col.	column
Coll.	*Collections*
Dist	*District*
Doc.	*Documents*
Eccles.	*Ecclesiastical*
Ecol.	*Ecological; Ecology*
Econ.	*Economic; Economy*
edn	edition
Eng.	*England; English*
fig./figs	figure/figures
Fld	*Field*
fn.	footnote
fol./fols	folio/folios
Geog.	*Geographical; Geography*
Geol.	*Geological; Geology*
Hist.	*Historian; Historical; History*
Ind.	*Industrial; Industry*
Inst.	*Institute*
Jour.	*Journal*
Leg.	*Legal*
Mag.	*Magazine*
ms., mss	manuscript, manuscripts
Med.	*Medieval*
Misc.	*Miscellany*
Mod.	*Modern*
Mus.	*Museum*
n.d.	no date
n.s.	New Series
N&Q	*Notes & Queries*
Occas.	*Occasional*
o.s.	Old Series
p./pp.	page/pages
Pam.	*Pamphlets*
Pap.	*Papers*
pt./pts	part/parts

---

[1] In references numerals are often used: '17th cent.', instead of 'seventeenth century'.

pl./pls	plate/plates
Pop.	*Population*
Proc.	*Proceedings*
Publ.	*Publications*
Rec.	*Record; Records*
Rel.	*Religion; Religious*
Rept	*Report*
Res.	*Research*
Rev.	*Review*
Roy.	*Royal*
ser.	series
Sociol.	*Sociological; Sociology*
Soc.	*Society*
Stud.	*Studies*
supp.	supplement
Trans	*Transactions*
Univ.	*University*
vol./vols	volume/volumes
Yearbk	*Yearbook*

Examples:

Agrar. Hist. Eng. and Wales	*Agrarian History of England and Wales*
Econ. Hist. Rev.	*Economic History Review*
Jour. Eccles. Hist.	*Journal of Ecclesiastical History*
Local Pop. Stud.	*Local Population Studies*

Notes:

Place-names, names of counties and personal names should normally be spelled without abbreviation:

Trans Halifax Antiq. Soc.	*Transactions of the Halifax Antiquarian Society*
Sussex Archaeol. Coll.	*Sussex Archaeological Collections*
Trans Thoroton Soc.	*Transactions of the Thoroton Society*

A FEW EXCEPTIONS

Certain well-known sources, or those used repeatedly in a particular study, are often referred to simply by initials:

VCH	for *Victoria County History*
DNB	for *Dictionary of National Biography*
REED	for *Records of Early English Drama*
TLH	for *The Local Historian*
JORALS	for *Journal of Regional & Local Studies.*

It is of course necessary to explain such acronyms in a special 'key' (see p. viii, above).

Appendix 22

COMPILING A GLOSSARY

Readers of all kinds, ranging from general to highly specialist, can find valuable guidance and stimulation in well-constructed glossaries.[1] The purpose is, of course, to explain the forms and meanings of words in historical sources. Nearly all record publications need glossaries, even those dealing with 19th- and 20th-century texts. Furthermore, writers of secondary books and articles could include glossaries more frequently, especially when they have used technical, legal and other specialised terms which will not be familiar to all their readers (for example, 'crown-post', 'headborough', 'navigation', 'First Fruits' and 'Incorporated Hundred'). While some editors and authors miss these opportunities altogether, the glossaries which do appear in print are often inadequate — even in volumes issued by well-respected record societies.

The following steps need to be considered in compiling a glossary. The first two are essential, and the rest depend on the individual case:

1. If a word was spelt in several different ways, as often happens, give the variants in alphabetical order, e.g. HEYER, HEYIR, HEYYR (hair). However, one sometimes has too many variants to include them all, in which case it is important to give those which effect the first syllable or two, e.g. MAUZEY, MAWZYN (Malmsey wine). Major variations in the spelling of the first syllable may well necessitate the use of cross-references, e.g. STYKKES: see 'Stekes'.

2. If the old spelling of a word is different from today's, always give the modern equivalent before attempting a definition, e.g. MESTELYN: maslin … This is often forgotten, yet it is the vital key for readers who want to pursue the subject further.

3. A definition or explanation of the word, such as you might find in a dictionary, is frequently needed, e.g. MESTELYN: maslin, a mixture of wheat and rye. Make sure that you give the definition which is strictly relevant to the usage in your text. Do not merely copy everything the dictionary says about a particular word.

4. If a word was used in more than one sense, each must be carefully distinguished, e.g. STOUNE: 1. stone (e.g. as building material); 2. mill-stone; 3. measure of weight, which varies by commodity from 8 to 24 lbs, but often 14 lbs.

---

[1] In a book glossaries can appear before or after the text, more commonly the latter.

5.   If a word appears once or only occasionally in the original document or record publication, one should help the interested reader by giving references to the relevant page(s) or folio(s), e.g. HODE: wood (131v).

6.   Where a word is rare or specially important, one should similarly give helpful references to dictionaries and word-lists which yield the necessary explanations, e.g. TWIDDLES: pimples; a Suffolk term (Halliwell).

7.   If you make purely editorial comments, put them in square brackets. It is astonishing how many historical words, English and Latin, apparently mean 'unidentified' and 'obscure'!

Finally, give thought to the typography, punctuation and layout of your glossary, so that it is clear and attractive. With the help of a word-processor, it is particularly easy to experiment with such details.

HISTORICAL DATING

Answers to Exercises on pp. 105-6

1. 24 August
2. 27 April
3. 21 October or 22 August
4. 20 June
5. Thursday after Trinity Sunday (moveable)
6. 20 November 1275-19 November 1276
7. 22 June 1397—21 June 1398
8. 22 April 1546—28 January 1547
9. 29 May 1660—29 January 1661 (the reign of Charles II began on 30 January 1649 when his father was executed)
10. 5 April 1309
11. 6 September 1336
12. 20 October 1397
13. 27 August 1460
14. 31 January 1376 (leap year)
15. 9 January 1705 (New Style)

'I say this only, next to the immediate discharge of my Holy Office, I know not how in any course of studies I could have better served my patron, my people and my successors, than by preserving the memoirs of this parish and the adjacent parts, which before lay remote from common notice, and in a few years had been buried in unsearchable oblivion. If the present age be too immers'd in cares or pleasures, to take any relish or to make any use of these discoveries, I then appeal to posterity. For I believe the times will come when persons of better inclination will arise, who will be glad to find any collection of this nature, and will be ready to supply the defects, and carry on the continuation of it.'

(White Kennett, vicar of Ambrosden, Oxfordshire, wrote these timeless words in the earliest published history of an English parish: *Parochial Antiquities of Ambrosden, Burcester and Other Adjacent Parts*, (1695), pp. v-vi)

INDEX

Note that many items are grouped under the following main headings: **documents**; **local historians**; **local history**; **publishing**; **references**; **transcription**; **writing**. Place-names (except for those in greater London) are indented under the appropriate county.